AYURVEDA PANCHAKARMA

(Five purification procedures)

Indian Medical Science Series No. 101

AYURVEDA PANCHAKARMA

(Five purification procedures)

by :

Prof. Dr. P. H. Kulkarni

- ***Former Dean, Faculty of Ayurvedic Medicine, University of Pune***
- ***Ayurveda Reseearch guide, University of Pune***
- ***Director, Ayurveda Academy & Institute of Indian Medicine***

Sri Satguru Publications
A Division of
Indian Books Centre
Delhi, India

Published by
Sri Satguru Publications,
Indological and Oriental Publishers
A Division of
Indian Books Centre
40/5, Shakti Nagar,
Delhi-110007
India

Email: ibcindia@ibcindia.com
Website: http://www.ibcindia.com/
Assisted by: Dr.Mrs.Pradnya Akkalkotkar,
Dr.Mrs.Vineeta Bendale
Dr.Mahesh Sabade

First Edition; Pune 1999
Second Edition; Delhi, 2000

ISBN 81-7030-665-5

Published by Sunil Gupta for Sri Satguru Publications, a division of Indian Books Centre, 40/5, Shakti Nagar, Delhi-110007, India and printed at Chawla Offset Press, Delhi 110 052

SHREE DHANVANTAREE

श्री धन्वंतरी

This book is
Dedicated to all
Students of Ayurveda Panchakarma
in all continents of the world.

P. H. Kulkarni

Foreword

Study of Ayurveda is eternal. One can try to understand Ayurveda in one's life. It seems very difficult. Hence it is beneficial to study Ayurveda everyday, every life.

Whatever, I understood about Ayurveda, during last 44 years, I tried to write it. In this book salient features about various aspects of Panchakarma are considered as described in Ayurvedic Treaties and recent advances are considered for benefit of interested persons.

Hand book of Ayurvedic treatment, Ayurveda Kitchen (cooking), Ayurvedic massage, Ashtang Ayurveda and such other books are in press.

Let Ayurveda help every body to be always happy !

P. H. Kulkarni

London

U.K.

May - 1999

INDEX

1.
INTRODUCTION

1. Introduction

History of Panchakarma

In the history of Panchakarma we get references from the time of the Rugveda (one of the four Vedas). In the period of Gautam Buddha Panchakarma was well in practice. Lord Buddha also used to practice Panchakarama. He had given Raktamokshan to Pillindwachha, vaman to the king of Ujjain - Pradyota.

In the period of Charak and Sushrut, Panchakarma therapy was much flourished. Other authors like Vagbhat, Bhel, Kashyap, Sharangdhar have also described Panchakarma very elaborately in their texts. Similar therapies were in practice in Greece, Egypt, South America etc. in the past. In the period of Hippocrates, physicians used to administer different kinds of enemas.

Introduction of Panchakarma

Ayurve da has eight branches viz. - Kayachikitsa, Kaumarbhritya tantra, Grahachikitsa, Shalakya tantra, Shalya tantra, Visha tantra, Rasayan and Vajikaran.

Kayachikitsa (medicine), basically has two branches-Shaman (alleviation) and Shodhan (elimination). In any pathogenesis, there is imbalance of doshas which causes vitiation of dhatus and/ or malas. Shaman is the method of treating the disease without eliminating doshas out of the body, whereas shodhan is the method of eliminating vitiated doshas out of the body.

Both shodhan and shaman can be achieved by the fivefold therapy in Ayurveda called 'PANCHAKARMA'. These five procedures are :- Vaman (emesis), Virechan (purgation), Basti (medicated enemas), Nasya (errhine therapy) and Rakta mokshan (blood letting).

Vaman : This is the procedure of eliminating doshas from the upper orifice of the alimentary canal i.e. mouth. This is the first and the foremost karma (treatment) in Panchakarma. This procedure is commonly used for the treatment of kapha or kapha predominant diseases. 'Elimination of doshas should be done from the nearest route.' This is a basic principle. The Mouth being the nearest route to the aamashaya (stomach), which is the basic site of kaphadosha, vaman is the best indicated procedure for elimination of kapha dosha.

Virechan : In this procedure the vitiated doshas are eliminated through the lower orifice of the alimentary canal i.e. anus. This procedure is commonly used for pitta/pitta-predominant diseases.

Basti : This is the treatment in which medicated enemas are given. This is not just to clean the large intestine but also to avail different benefits.

These are basically of three kinds.

- Nirooha Basti: In which decoction of herbs is mainly used.
- Anuvasan Basti: In which sneha (unctous material like ghee, oil, milk) is mainly used.
- Uttar Basti: This is a kind of basti given in the bladder through the urethra for both the sexes and in the uterus through vaginal orifice for females.

Nasya: This is a procedure in which the medicines are administered through the nasal route. The Nose is the approach to the interior of the head, therefore the medicines given through nose are effective in the head diseases (headache due to various reasons) and various diseases above the sternal notch.

Raktamokshan : This is the method of blood letting. It may be stated that by oozing the blood outside the body, the raktavaha srotas (spleen and liver) gets stimulated to produce better quality of raktadhatu. (Panchakarama can be done for these three objectives-)

- To maintain the health.
- Prior to Rasayan and Vajikaran treatments to give more benefits of these two therapies.
- For the treatment of diseases.

Introduction of Aam : Various factors like overeating, intake of mutually contradictory food, irregular food timings etc. lead to Agnimaandya (suppression of digestive power). Hence the rasa dhatu (first dhatu) remains undigested. This undigested rasa dhatu gets vitiated in the Aamashay and is termed as Aam.

When the doshas are vitiated by this aam, they are termed as saam doshas and these saam doshas further lead to various diseases. Hence the alleviation and elimination of such doshas is very necessary.

One of the basic principles of Ayurvedic treatment is that doshas should never be eliminated in the saam condition, as in this saam condition it is very difficult to separate the doshas from the internal surface of the body/organs where they are situated and may cause harm to the body surface, if tried so. This is due to the styaan, pichhil properties of aam.

Hence alleviation of aam is very important which helps in achieving the niraam (without aam) condition of doshas. This is the right stage for the expulsion of the vitiated doshas. For alleviation of aam, the power of digestion should be increased. For this purpose the line of treatment that should be used is Langhan and Paachan.

Introduction of Langhan and Paachan : Langhan (limited intake of light food / complete fasting) helps in increasing the digestive power. Paachan is digestion. Various internal medicines and process such as rooksha swedan (dry fomentation) are used for this purpose. This therapy helps in digestion of aam and hence leads to increase the digestive power.

Role of Snehan and Swedan in Panchakarma : According to Ayurveda the disease is the state in which vitiated doshas go to the deeper levels in the body (from koshtha to shakha). The basic aim of the treatment is to bring the vitiated doshas to the superficial level (from shakha to koshtha) and then to eliminate them through the nearest outlet. This is shodan.

This state of accumulating vitiated doshas in koshtha is achieved by snehan (oleation) and swedan (fomentation). Snehan and swedan help in the detachment of doshas from their substractum and accumulation of doshas in the koshtha. Hence paachan, snehan and swedan play an important role in the poorvakarma of any pachakarma. As there is the elimination of vitiated doshas from the body, the chances of recurrence of the disease are very remote.

If one wants to undergo all the procedures in panchakarma, the sequence should be as follows :

Vaman for 9 days (including poorvakarma and pashchatkarama).

Virechan on 15th day after vaman is completed.

Basti on 9th day after virechan is completed, basti Course should be started (30 days in case of karma basti and in case of yoga/kal basti the period will vary accordingly).

Total days are 62 days.

Dietetic and behavioral regime should be followed for twice the number of days of basti course i.e. Hence 62 + 60 =122 days. After basti 7 days for Nasya = 129 and then on the 9th day raktamokshan should be done. This way generally it takes around 138 days for all the procedures in Panchakarma.

History of Ayurveda

Ayurveda originated before human beings. Scriptures say that the whole of nature was generated by Lord Brahma and Lord Brahma himself, recalled Ayurveda. Among vedas, Rugveda and Atharvaveda have described Ayurveda. Ayurveda is said to be the subtype of Atharvaveda, as much of Ayurveda is explained in it.

One can get many references about Ayurveda in ancient religious texts like Smrutis, Ramayana, Mahabharata etc. There were many great physicians, as well as surgeons who used to treat various diseases. Ashwinikumar, DakshaPrajapati, Bhel, Jatukarna, Ravan, Parashar, etc. were few of them. There are references even of the transplantation of testes, preservation of dead bodies and treatment of many diseases. Ravan was an authority on Nadishastra. Lord Buddha also had the knowledge of Ayurveda and used to practise Ayurveda.

Charak Samhita and Sushrut Samhita - The basic texts for Ayurveda were written in the period 1000 - 1500 BC. Ashtang Sangraha was written in 6th century by Vagbhatacharya. Charak Samhita, Sushrut Samhita and Ashtang Sangraha together is called as Bruhattrayi Madhavnidan, Sharangdhar Samhita and Bhavaprakash together is called Laghutrayi. Madhavnidan was written in the 7th century; Sharagdhar Samhita in the 13th and Bhavaprakash in the 16 th century. In the period of these texts, Ayurveda was a flourished science. In the period of Bouddha religion, the followers of Lord Buddha propagated their religion and Ayurveda in the neighbouring countries. After that there were many ups and downs of progress in different branches of Ayurveda.

Introduction of Ayurveda

Ayurveda literally means the science of life. It is the natural healing system of India. It is a boon to mankind and has originated as a part of vedic science. This ancient medical science has its roots deep in vedic philosophy. Ayurveda believes and emphasizes that whatever is present in the macrocosm is also present in the individual body in a miniature form and hence the study of nature becomes an integral part of it.

Dhanvantari, an incarnation of Lord Vishnu is the divine consciousness which represents the truth in the tradition of Ayurveda. The Vedic system including Ayurveda was in practice 4000 B.C. This is the world's oldest and the richest source of natural healing systems. The scriptures say that Ayurveda was recalled by Lord Brahma (which means it was omni present) and then it was taught by Lord Brahma to the other followers. It doesn't deal only with the medicine but also with the way of living, the basic aims of life which are Dharma, Artha, Kama & Moksha. Dharma is to follow the spiritual, social and moral tenets and duties towards the self and others.

Artha is to earn a livelihood.

Kama Comprises all kinds of desires.

Moksha means salvation i.e., to break the cycle of birth-death and rebirth. The Word Ayurveda comprises Ayu or (life) and Veda or (science). Ayu is defined as a combination of sharir (body), indriya (senses), satva (mind), atma (soul) and Ayurveda is the study of all these.

The whole universe along with macrocosm or (human body) is purely based on the five primordial elements. These are prithvi (earth), aap (water), tej (fire), vayu (air) and aakash (ether). These five elements are called the PANCHAMAHABHUTAS. Each and every substance in this universe is composed of these five elements but the only difference is in their proportion e.g., in milk aap mahabhut is more than the other four; and in any metal Prithvi mahabhut forms the major part.

The human body is composed of three doshas (humors), seven dhatus and three malas (excreta). Vata, pitta and kapha are the three basic biological humors which conduct the body functions. Rasa, rakta, mansa, meda, asthi, majja and shukra are seven dhatus which hold the body for the basic functions. And purish (stools), mutra (urine) and sweda (sweat) are the basic malas (excreta). These malas also play a major role in performing body functions. Various etiological factors vitiate the doshas (one or more). Doshas then vitiate the dhatus or, malas leading to the manifestation of the diseases. If all these constituents along with the soul, mind sense organs are in equilibrium and in good health, then and only then can the individual referred to as a healthy person.

❖❖❖

2.
SNEHAN & SWEDAN

2. Snehan & Swedan

The meaning of the term snehan is oleation i.e., to oleate the body internally and / or externally. Swedan is fomentation. Various types of swedan have been described in Ayurvedic texts. Both these therapies can be used separately, either independently as the main therapy or as a poorva-karma (pre-operative therapy) of the pradhan-karma (main procedure).

Snehan

Snehan as Pradhan Karma (main therapy):

External and / or internal snehan can be administered to achieve following benefits:

1. Snehan helps in alleviation of vata. Properties of sneha to dravyas (substances) are exactly the opposite that of vata and hence sneha is the best antidote of vata.
2. Sneha dravyas lead to the softening of doshas.
3. Sneha increases Agni (power of digestion).
4. It strengthens the body by stimulating the genearation of dhatus.
5. Longivity is achieved due to good strength of dhatus by snehan.
6. Snehan enhances the functioning of Indriyas (sense organs).
7. Immunity of the body is increased due to increased Agni and increased strength of dhatus by snehan.

Snehan as poorva-karma (pre-operative procedure) :
Importance of snehan as a poorva-karma has been emphasized in various Ayurvedic texts. Snehan helps in softening of doshas and separating them from their substratum, which is necessary procedure for elimination of doshas from the body.

Some examples have been given to elaborate this action of snehan:

1. If water contained in a vessel oleated from inside is poured out, all the water rushes out of the vessel without a single drop of water remaining inside, similarly complete elimination of doshas is achieved with the help of shehan as a poorva-karma.
2. As soap is used to separate the dirt form the clothes, similarly snehan is performed for complete separation of doshas from their subsrtatum.

Swedan :

Swedan as pradhan karma :

1. Alleviation of vata due to the opposite properties of swedan dravyas to that of vata.
2. Stiffness in any part of the body is alleviated by swedan as stiffness is one of the symptoms of vitiated vata.
3. Ushna (hot) and (Penetrating) Teekshna properties of swedan dravyas help in the digestion of aam subsequently increasing the Agni (power of digestion).
4. Texture and complexion of skin is improved due to swedan.

Swedan as a poorva-karma :

Snehan is followed by swedan in any poorva-karma. Swedan helps in separation of doshas from their substratum and their collection in koshtha. Vata plays an important role in directing the doshas towards the koshtha and proper direction of vata is achieved by swedan. Thus, the doshas are collectively brought in the koshtha with the help of snehan and swedan for their elimination by any eliminative therapy of panchakarma.

3.
PANCHAKARMA & YOU

3. Panchakarma and you

To maintain the health

One of the basic principles of Ayurveda is to maintain the health of the healthy persons and to cure the diseases. The phrase 'Prevention is better than cure' is well known. This principle of Ayurveda goes hand in hand with the same. Panchakarma helps to maintain the health mainly by following the 'Dinacharya' and 'Rutucharya' i.e., the daily regimen and the seasonal regimen.

Use of following therapies daily helps one to maintain the health.

1. Abhyang (oleation).
2. Udvartan (Rubbing of dry medicated powders).
3. Shiro-abhyang (applicaion of the oil on head)
4. Prati-marsha Nasya (administration of medicines via the nasal route)
5. Matra-basti (administration of medicated/plain oil via the anal route).
6. Karna-puran (administration of oil in the ears).
7. Shiro-pichu Dharan (keeping a piece of cotton soaked in the oil on the head).
8. Gandusha and Kawal Dharan (gargles or retaining medicated oils/decoction/ghee in oral cavity)
9. Dhoomapan (medicinal smoke inhalation).

Panchakarma in Seasonal Regimen (Rutucharya) :

Man has to struggle continuosly against his ever-changing environment to keep himself fit and in the best of his health in all the seasons. By following the rules described in the seasonal regimen, the continuous interaction and adjustment between the internal and external environmental factors of man is made easier. This helps the individuals to keep themselves fit in the changing seasons.

The effect of the seasons on the three Doshas (Vata, Pitta, & Kapha) has been described in this table.

Dosha	Varsha Monsoon	Sharad Autumn	Hemant Early Winter	Shishir Late Winer	Vasant Spring	Grishma Summer
Vata	++	0				+
Pitta	+	++	0			
Kapha				+	++	0

++: Prakopa (provokation) of the particular dosha in the body in the particular season.
+: Chaya (accumulation) of the particualar dosha in the body in the particular season.
0: Prasham (pacification) of the particular dosha in the body in the particular season.
NB: The above chart is according to the opinion of Vagabhatta.

Panchakarma in various seasons

Karma	Varsha Monsoon	Sharad Autumn	Hemant Early Winter	Shishir Late Winer	Vasant Spring	Grishma Summer
Snehan	Vata shamak (alleviating) oils	Ghee medicated with pittashamak (alleviating) medicines	Warm oil medicated with vatashama K (alleviating) medicines	Same as in Hemant	Hot oil medicated with Kaphasha mak (alleviating) medicines	Ghee medicated with vata & pitta Shamak (alleviating) medicines
Swedan	Rooksha	Mild Sweda	Snigdha	Snigdha sweda	Rooksha sweda	Mild or may not be given
Vaman	Contra-indicated	Contra-indicated	Contra-indicated	Contra-indicated	Advised	Contra-indicated

Virech-ana	Mrudu Virechana	Advised	Contra-indicated	Contra-indicated	If advised by Vaidya	*
Basti	Advised	Contra-indicated	Contra-indicated	Contra-indicated	Nirooha Basti	*
Rakta-moksh-ana	Contra-indicated	Advised	Contra-indicated	Contra-indicated	Contra-indicated	Contra-indicated
Nasya	Contra-indicated	Contra-indicated	Contra-indicated	Contra-indicated	Advised	Contra-indicated

*: Can be performed by the consent of vaidyas.

The above chart shows the panchakarma that should be performed in various rutus (seasons) in healty persons. But, the various karmas can be performed in any season in diseased condition only by the advice of the vaidyas.

Panchakarma in Rasayan & Vajikaran Chikitsa (treatment):

Rasayan is defined as tonic,which promotes health, well being by improving the quality of all the tissues. Vajikar dravyas (substances) have a marked action on sexual sphere and organs.

The Rasayan and Vajikaran chikitsa have been described in detail in the Ayurvedic texts. But prior to that, it is necessary that body is purified with the help of panchamkarma. The complete results of Rasayan and Vajikaran are achieved only after the panchakarma treatment is done as it purifies the body by elimination and alleviation.

To cure the diseases

Ayurvedic treatment has been classified in various ways. One of the classifications is shodhan and shaman. Shodan chikitsa includes complete elimination of vitiated doshas and shaman chikitsa pacifies the doshas. As the vitiated doshas are completely eliminated from the body, prior to shaman chikitsa, the disease is completely cured and the chances of recurrence of the disease are very remote. The shodhan chikitsa is done with the aid of panchakarma i.e., shiro-virechan nasya etc.

Beauty and Panchakarma

Panchakarma and some allied karmas are of great value in maintainance and the improvement of one's beauty. While thinking about beauty, the main features to be considered are good-complexion, attractive personality, attractive hair and eyes.

Good Complexion : Abhyang helps to achieve good complexion by improving the blood circulation and also by doing vata-prashaman [skin is one of the sthana (site) of vata dosha and vitiated vata dosha creates dryness and blackishness of the skin].

Hair : Shiro-abhyang, shiro-dhara, shiro-basti and nasya help in stoping the hair-fall, graying of hair and certainly improving the quality of the hair.

Eyes : Long and dense eyelashes are the true make-up of eyes, which can be achieved naturally, with the help of netra-tarpana (filling medicated oil/ghee over the eyes for a certain period). Spectacles may become a negative point in the personality of a person.

Netra tarpan helps in achieving proper vision without the help of spectacles.

Attractive Personality : Proper tone and shape of specific organs can be achieved with the help of Abhyang.

Regular Abhyang with medicated oils helps in increasing the weight of those who are too thin.

Over weight persons can attain weight reduction with the aid of swedan.

Feet : Padabhyang is successfully performed to cure the cracked soles.

Stress and Panchakarma :

Stress has become an inseparable factor of the modern world. The reasons of stress may vary from person to person like stress due to family problems, financial, health, the social problems etc. Stress leads to various health problems like diseases of the Gastro-intestinal tract, insomnia, graying of hair fall, hampering the quality of skin complexion etc.

Panchakarma, along with some allied karmas is of definite use in resolving the stress-induced problems. Diseases of the Gastro-intestinal tract like hyperacidity, constipation, anorexia; etc can be treated accordingly with the help of vaman, virechan and basti. Shiro-abhyang, shiro-dhara, shiro-basti and padabhyang are very successfully performed to treat insomnia.

The problems related with hair and skin have been discussed previously in the point ' Beauty and Panchakarma'.

Today's life and Panchakarma :

The pattern of daily regimen (Dinacharya) that has been described in the Ayurvedic texts is practically very diffcult to follow in today's busy life-style. But still, maintainance of health is the most important point to be achieved, if one has to cope up with the hectic life-pattern. Hence, one must find time for himself/or herself to perform atleast some of the procedures described in the texts, which are as follows.

Abyang : Application of oil the to the body prior to the bath (especially to the head, ears and feet).

Shiro-Abhyang : Oil application on the head atleast twice a week, if not daily/.

Prati-marsha Nasya

Matra-basti.

About Constitution

Prakruti

Ayurvedic treatment is based upon the ascertainment of indivdual constitution. This is the unique power of the system in which it treats the living individual as the most important factor. Ayurveda does not regard disease as a factor in itself but only as a complication of imbalance of doshas. Hence it regards more as a product of how we live than as an attack from the outside.

The predominance of the elements, gunas decide the physical constitution of an individual. Once this proportion is set it remains permanent for the lifetime of an individual. The prakruti or physical constitution of an individual depends upon the following :

Condition of sperm and ovum at the time of conception.

Nature of the season and the condition inside the uterus.

Food and other regimens adapted by mother during pregnancy.

The predominance of doshas determines the functional or doshic prakruti, the energetic condition of the body. Of these types of constitution, the classification of dominance of doshas is most important in the examination of both the health and the disease.

Functional or Doshic Constitution :

Based on the permutations and combinations of the three doshas, seven types of constitutions can be formed:

Vata

Pitta

Kapha

Vata-pitta

Vata-kapha

Pitta-kapha

Sannipata or balanced constition (sama prakruti)

These types are classified by their predominance. We find that a purely single dosha constituion is seldom found and although a balanced constitution is extremely good, this type is also rare.

Vata constitution is usually inferior in terms of health and longevity; Pitta is usually in between; and kapha is usually superior. Of the dual constitutions pitta-kapha type is good in terms of health and longevity as compared to vata-kapha type, which in turn is better than vata-pitta type.

Importance of Constitution :

If we observe different individuals and their nutritional requirements, their tolerance to the atmosphere or their behaviour patterns we find that for maintaining health they have different needs. They may prefer different types of food, drink and activity. Even in two people with identical weight and height, their requirements vary. One may prefer large amount of food or drink, while the other may prefer less. If we analyse the serum or blood in these individuals, we may not find any substantial difference. Yet differences clearly exist. Therefore, it becomes clear that tolerance to food, drink or environment can not be decided by the analytical study of the body tissues. It depends upon the individual constitution. By understanding the constitution of every individual, we know which food and drink and what type of job and exercise is appropriate for maintaining his or her health.

As there is a predominance of dosha in each individual, each type requires substances different or opposite to the constitution to maintain health. Vata people posses qualities of coldness, dryness, roughness and lightness. Hence a person of vata constitution requires substances which are warm or hot, oily or unctuous. Otherwise, there is always a tendency of vata to increase, giving rise to vata diseases. To compensate for the vata in his constitution, he should eat food having sweet, sour and salty tastes. For maintanance of health, every person should know his or her constitution. We have seen that in each constitution there is a predominance of one or more doshas. If the daily activities, diet, occupation and behaviour are not adjusted to balance this, then the constitutional doshas will increase, thus giving rise to its characteristic diseases. If the constitution is known then medicines, diet and other regimens including yogic postures can be advised correctly, both, for disease treatment and to promote longevity.

Psychological Constitution :

This is decided according to which of the three gunas is dominant at the time of birth.

Satvic constitution :

These individuals possess a good intellect and memory and have an inherent instinct for cleanliness. Although they tend to possess a great deal of knowledge, they will always make efforts to gain more. Then they have a good will and allow others to prosper. They are polite, have faith in the divine and devotion to the God.

Rajas Constitution :

Rajas types have a nature that tries to overpower the others. They manifest a propulsive and dynamic energy. They are not satisfied with the positions and possessions they achieve and therefore, always strive for more.

Hence they are ambitious and industrious in nature. Usually these people are hot tempered and egoistic. They over express pain or pleasure. They have a brave but jealous and cruel character.

Tamas Constitution :

These persons are lazy and ignorant. Similarly, they are not curious about anything. Usually they have less intelligence, prefer not to work and are interested in eating and sleeping. They avoid cleanliness and are not health conscious. They are afraid of many things, hence they do not initiate any work on their own.

Vata Prakruti :

These people usually have tall or thin bodily frames and less strength. Their body weight is low and they have less resistance to the disease. The digestion and metabolism is variable and changeable, hence they can not form sturdy and stable tissues. Their life span is usually shorter than other individuals. Because of this variable nature, they can not perform their tasks steadily and continuously. Hence they may fail in achieving their goals or become involved in side tracks to them. Such individuals require a job with less strenous physical activity, where constant attention is not required and which is not in a cold or dry atmosphere. If they are forced to undertake such work, they are likely to become subject to the disease of the nerves and bones and various diseases due to vitiation of vata.

Pitta Prakruti :

These persons have quick and rapid digestive and metabolic activity. Hence they require constant food and drinks which are cool and unctuous in nature. They are able to convert food to a good quality of tissue, but as the total conversion rate in the body is very fast they also usually have shorter life spans when compared to kapha types. They have soft, oily and smooth skin. They tend to become bald at an early age and their hair become gray prematurely. They have moderate strength and capacity to work although they are hot tempered. They have good grasping power and are very intelligent. They usually possess good knowledge in their chosen subjects, are creative in nature and often possess wealth and status in society.

These persons require a job in a cool atmosphere, with some creative activity and intelligent work.

Kapha Prakruti :

These persons possess hefty, robust and thick body frames, with stout musculature. They naturally possess good strength, immunity, vitality and are thus generally healthy and have a longer life span. They have smooth and deep voices and are often good looking. The total digestive and metabolic rate in these individuals is very slow, hence they require less food or drinks. They are of a calm and quiet nature.

Kapha types can carry out work that is heavy or strenuous. They are also good in maintaining public relations. However, they should not work in cold and damp atmospheres. They are likely to become obese and may fall victim to joint diseases and heart problems.

❖❖❖

4.
VAMAN

4. Vaman

Poorvakarma :

Pre-operative

a) Snehan : It is administered in two ways.

I) Bahya (external) - External application of oil or sneha is called 'Bahya snehan.'

II) Abhyantara Snehana (internal oleation) : Intake of plain or medicinal ghee or oil through the mouth, in an increasing dose is called 'Abhyantara snehana.'

According to body types - per 3 days for - Kapha prakruti

5 days for - Pitta prakruti and

7 days for - Vata prakruti

The time periods have been explained in the text. But criteria for the completion of snehan, should be observed along with the mentioned time periods.

Rules of snehan e.g. drinking warm water etc. should be followed for the whole period of snehan.

a) Swedan : Snehan will be followed by swedan (fomentation). Usually a steam bath is taken for this purpose.

b) Instruments Used : Glasses, jars, tubs, measuring glass, napkins or towels, burner, plates, apron etc.

c) Medicines used : various vaman dravyas (medicines used for vaman) have been described in the different texts. The list of medicines, that are mainly used has been given.

Madanphala	Randia dumatorum
Vacha	Acorus calamus
Yashtimadhu	Glycerrhiza glabra

Saindhav	Rock salt
Ela	Elettaria cardamoum
Pippali	Piper longum
Kutaj	Holarrhena antidysenterica
Jeemootak	Luffa echinata

Matra (Dose) of vaman dravyas :

1. It differs in various individuals
2. Ideal dose is that :

a) Which helps in the removal of maximum vitiated doshas while the required dose is minimum.

b) Which causes proper bouts.

c) Which is digested easily.

d) Which will have the property to alleviate the disease.

e) Which is convenient to take.

When the strength of the disease and agni (digestive power) is medium, the dose of the decoction to be administered to the patient is one Anjali (4 pala - 16 tolas - 160 gms approx.)

Pradhan Karma :

1) After completion of internal snehan (oleation) a gap of one day is given. Patient should not take internal sneha on that day. External snehan - swedan should be done. On the previous day, for the dinner patient should have food which aggravates kapha dosha e.g. curd, ghee, rice etc.

2) On the day of vaman, patient should not have any food in the morning prior to vaman. Some times peya and ghee is given for aggravation of kapha dosha and internal lubrication.

3) On the next day, the procedure of vaman should be performed early in the morning i.e. in the kapha kala i.e. approximately from 6 a.m. to 9.30 a.m.

4) The Patient should be calm and quiet and he should be convinced that the procedure is for the betterment of his health. This helps for the procedure to be carried out smoothly.

5) The patient who has undergone oleation and fomentation must be made to sit on a stool, which has a height upto the knee.

6) The following medicines are prepared in a powder form and given to the patient along with the honey in the dose of 5 to 10 gms.

Madan phala (Randia dumatorum) - 4 parts.

Vacha (Acorus calamus) - 2 parts.

Saindhav (Rock salt) - 1 part.

After that decoction of Yashtimadhu i.e. (Glycerrhiza glabra) or sugar-cane juice is given to the patient in the maximum dose.

7) The patient should be observed after the administration of the medicines. The first effect would be perspiration, which indicates that the doshas have started loosening from their position. Secondly, Perspiration is observed which indicates that the doshas have started moving from their positions. The third stage consists of distention of the abdomen, which indicates that the doshas have reached the intestines. Fourthly nausea and salivation indicate the upward movement of doshas towards the mouth.

8) The patient should be instructed to vomit in the vessel kept in front of him. Two persons should stay on either side and hold the sides of his fore head and massage his back.

If the bouts do not start, they should be induced either with mechanical means i.e. by stimulating with the touch of a lotus stem or (kamal naal) to the throat or vomiting can be induced by giving mixture of, pippali, Amalaki, sarshapa and Vacha or lukewarm water and salt.

Pashchat Karma :

1. Criteria for completion of Vaman :

The completion of vaman is studied on the basis of 4 norms.

a) Aantiki : i.e., the dosha, which is expelled at the end of vaman i.e. pitta or kapha Kshaya (alleviation of kapha dosha) should be observed.

b) Maniki : i.e. the quantity of vomitus which is graded according to maximum, medium and minimum quantity i.e. 256 tolas (2560 gms approx.), 192 tolas (1920 gms approx) and 128 tolas (1280 gms approx) respectively.

c) Vegiki : i.e., the number of bouts, which is again graded as maximum, medium and minimum as 8, 6 and 4 bouts respectively.

d) Laingiki : i.e. symptoms or condition of the patient at the end of vaman i.e.

i. The order of doshas passed :

Kapha

Pitta

ii. Feeling of lightness in the body.

iii. Weakness in the body.

iv. Clarity of mind.

v. Lightness in the sides of the chest, head and in the srotas.

Signs and symptoms of improper vaman (Ayoga)

i. Irregular bouts.

ii. Only medicine will be expelled. (thrown out)

iii. Heaviness in the body.

iv. Kotha (eruptions)

v. Fever

vi. Kandu (itching)

vii. Vibandha etc.

Signs and symptoms of excessive vaman (Atiyoga)

i. Thirst

ii. Blood stained vomiting (vomitus)

iii. Frothy vomiting

iv. Loss of strength

v. Vitiation of vata

vi. Chest pain

vii. Giddiness

viii. Burning sensation

ix. Expulsion of excessive pitta dosha.

x. Black outs etc.

2. Dhoomapan :

After completion of vaman, the patient should be advised to rest for about 48 minutes (one muhoorta). Later on Dhoomapan should be performed to clear the throat, mouth and nasal passages, which are obstructed by the residual kapha dosha.

3. Rules and regulations to be followed after vaman

Don'ts (Pariharya Vishay)

a. Speaking aloud

b. Over-eating

c. Standing for a long period

d. Resorting to anger and grief

e. Exposure to sun, stormy winds

f. Travelling by vehicles.

g. Indulging in sexual intercourse

h. Suppression of natural urges like passing of urine, stools etc.

i. Sleeping during day time

j. Vigil during the night

k. Intake of heavy diet.

Do's

Sansarjan Kram and other Karmas (Procedures) :

a. Sansarjan Kram : The mandaagni (decreased digestive power) already present must be stimulated, by giving light diet (laghu bhojan) and later on heavy diet (guru bhojan) gradually. The normal diet must be restored within 7 days. Peya, vilepi, akruta yusha, krutayusha, akruta maansa rasa and kruta maansa rasa must be given to a patient who has the shuddhi of pradhan, madhya and avaar accordingly. The normal diet must be restored on the third day to the avaar shuddhi patient; on fifth day for the patient having madhya shuddhi and on the seventh day to patient having pradhan shuddhi. By Following this procedure, the power of agni is increased in such a way that it is able to digest even the heavy food.

b. Tarpana and shamanoushadha : Instead of peya and vilepi, tarpana and shamanoushadha should be given in case of inadequate vaman or kapha pitta dominance. Peya aggravates kapha dosha. Hence instead of peya, mantha or yush should be given ahd instead of vilepi, ghana tarpana (ghana-thick) may be given.

Indications (disease)

i. Peenasa (nasal diseases)

ii. Kushtha (skin diseases)

iii. Navajwara (Acute fever)

iv. Kasa (cough)

v. Rajayakshma (Tuberculosis)

vi. Shwasa (asthma)

vii. Galaganda (goiter)

viii. Shleepada (elephantiasis)

ix. Prameha (diabetes)

x. Ajeerna (indigestion)

xi. Visoochika, Alasaka (Gastroenteritis)

xii. Vishapeeta (Poisoning)

xiii. Visha dushta (Poison)

xiv. Adhoga Raktapitta (bleeding through external orifices in the lower region of the body without any external injury).

xv. Arsha (Haemorrhoids)

xvi. Mukh praseka or Hrillasa (Nausea) (Exccessive Salivation prior to vomitting)

xvii. Aruchi, Avipaka (Anorexia etc.)

xviii. Unmada (insanity)

xix. Apasmara (epilepsy)

xx. Shopha (oedema)

xxi. Atisara (diarrhoea)

xxii. Mukhapaka (stomatitis) (ulcers in the month)

xxiii. Arbuda (tumour)

xxiv. Stanya dushti (vitiated breast milk)

xxv. Medoroga (0besity)

xxvi. Vidradhi (abscess)

xxvii. Kantha pak (pharyngitis)

xxviii. Vidarika

xxix. Hridroga (heart disease)

xxx. Visarpa (erysipelas)

xxxi. Putinasa (foul nasal odour)

xxxii. Karna srava (otorrhoea) (ear secretions)

xxxiii. Kapha vyadhi (kapha pre-dominant diseases) etc.

Contraindications :

i. Kśhatakshina (weakness due to injury)

ii. Atisthula (very obese)

iii. Atikrisha (very thin)

iv. Balaka (child)

v. Shranta (exhausted)

vi. Durbala (weak)

vii. Hungry & thirsty, fasting

viii. Excessive exercise, excessive sex indulgence, excessive study.

ix. Garbhini (pregnant lady)

x. Krimi koshtha (worm infestation)

xi. Urdhwaga raktapitta (Bleeding through external orifices in the upper region of the body without any external injury).

xii. Asthapita, anuvasita (after administration of basti)

xiii. Heart disease

xiv. Udavarta

xv. Mootragraha (retention of urine)

xvi. Pleeha dosha (splenic disorders)

xvii. Udara (ascitis)

xviii. Svaropaghata (voice impairment)

xix. Gulma (tumour)

xx. Ashtheela (prostate enlargement)

xxi. Timira (opthalmic disorder)

xxii. Sheera, karna shoola (head ache, earache)

5.
VIRECHAN

5. Virechan

Poorvakarma :

Pre- operative

a) Snehana : it is administered in two ways.

I) Bahya (external) - External application of oil or sneha is called Bahya snehan.

ii) Abhyantara Snehan (internal oleation) : Intake of plain or medicinal ghee or oil through the mouth in an increasing dose is called abhyantara snehana.

According to body types -

3 days for - Kapha prakruti

5 days for - Pitta prakruti and

7 days for - Vata prakruti

This time period have been explained in the text. But the criteria for completion of snehan should be observed along with the mentioned time periods. The Rules mentioned of snehan e.g. drinking warm water etc. should be followed for whole period of snehan.

Swedan : Snehan will be followed by swedan (fomentation) Usually steam bath is used for this purpose.

Matra Vinishchay (Dosage of drugs) :

In virechan, the digestion of the drug used for virechan is expected & it depends on Koshtha & Agni of the person. Agni is the digestive capacity of a person & Koshtha varies according to Agni.

In Mrudu Koshtha, pitta dosha is dominant & Agni is strong. Hence the dosage of Virechan drug should be less.

In Kroora Koshtha vata dosha is dominant & hence the capacity of Agni varies. In such cases strong dose of Virechan dravya should be administered.

In Madhyam Koshtha, capacity of Agni is medium & the dosage should be medium.

Hence while deciding the dosage of the drug the Koshtha of the patient & the potency of the drug should necessarily be considered.

Instruments used : Two towels

Virechan Dravyas

Other medicines as a precaution in case of improper virechan.

Pradhan Karma :

Administration of Virechan Yoga : The individual who has undergone Samyak snehan (proper oleation) and Swedan (Fomentation) should be selected for Virechan therapy.

After noting a good day, on confirming the digestion of previous meal & a good night's sleep, the patient with good mental control is given the virechan yoga early in the morning. Swasti vachaana (Holy rhymes) are also recited.

Generally the following prescription is given to the patient.

1. Draksha (Vitis vinfera Linn) - 1 Tola (10 gms)
2. Aragwadha (Cassia fistula Linn) - 1 Tola (10 gms)
3. Hareetaki (Terminalia chebula Linn) - 1 Tola (10 gms)
4. Katurohini (Picrorrhiza kurroa) - 1/2 Tola (5 gms)

Add these four drugs to 16 Tolas (160 gms) of water & boil it, till it reduce is to 1/4th. Administer 4 tolas (40 gms) of decoction along with 2.5 Tolas (25 gms) of Eranda Taila (Castor oil) and icchabhedi ras (500 mg) to the patient. This will induce teekshna (drastic) virechan. Icchabhedi must be given only when the decoction is cooled. If madhyam vegas (medium bouts) are expected then icchabhedi should not be given. If only jaghaanya vegas (minimum bouts) are required, then Virechan kwath is given to the patient to drink.

Pashchat Karma (Post operative procedure) :

Criteria for completion of Virechan : Excretion of stools, pitta and kapha in the proper sequence is the critera for completion of virechan. A Feeling of lightness and weakness are also the indications for the completion of proper virechan.

Proper or Improper Virechan :

Criteria for proper virechan : The completion of proper virechan is studied on the basis of four norms.

1. Vegiki i.e. the number of bouts.
2. Maniki i.e. the quantity of stools.
3. Aantiki i.e. the dosha which is excreted at the end of virechan.
4. Laingiki i.e. the condition of the patient at the end of virechan.

These 4 norms are further classified into three grades i.e. maximum, medium and minimum.

Pareeksha	Maximum	Medium	Minimum
Vaigiki	30 bouts	20 bouts	10 bouts
Maniki	4 prastha 216 tola (2160 gms approx.)	3 Prastha 116 tola (1160 gms. approx.)	2 Prastha 108 Tola (1080 gms. approx.)
Aantiki	Kaphant	Kaphant	Kaphant

Laingiki	Feeling of cleanliness in the channels and sense organs, lightness in the body and increase in digestive power (after some time).
Kaphant - Ending with kaph.	

Improper Virechan :

Signs and symptoms of improper or inadequate Virechan : (Ayoga)

Vitiation of kapha, pitta and vata, decrease in digestive power (agnimaandya), heaviness (gourav), coryza (pratishyay), drowsiness, vomitting (chhardi), eruptions (pidaka), anorexia (aruchi), obstruction to vata (vatapratilomata), burning sensation (daaha), heaviness (gourava) in the cardiac region and in the abdomen, itching and (kandu), constipation or obstruction to faeces (vishtambha), obstruction to the flow of urine (mootra sanga).

Signs and symptoms of excessive virechan : (Atiyoga)

Numbness (supti), bodyache (angamarda), exhaustion (Klama), tremors (kampa), sleep (nidra) and other symptoms originated by vata, fainting (moorchha), mental disturbance (unmad), hiccup (hikka), prolapse of rectum (gudabhransha), thirst (trishna), giddiness (bhrama) and blackouts (tamapravesha). The stools passed by the patient will be watery without kapha and pitta. The fluid may resemble the fluid, which remains after washing the meat, or it may have the colour of lohita (iron).

Sansarjan kram and other karmas (procedures) :.

a. Sansarjan Kram : The mandaagni (decreased digestive power) already present must be stimulated by giving a light diet (laghu bhojan) and later on a heavy diet (guru bhojan) gradually. The normal diet must be restored within 7 days. Peya, vilepi, akruta yusha, krutayusha, akruta maansa rasa and kruta maansa rasa must be given to a patient who has pradhan, madhya and avar Shuddhi accordingly. The normal diet must be restored on the third day to the avaar shuddhi patient; on fifth day to the patient with madhya shuddhi and on the seventh day to the patient with pradhan shuddhi. Following this procedure, the power of agni is increased in such a way that it is able to digest even the heavy food.

b. Tarpana and shamanoushadha : Instead of peya and vilepi, tarpana and shamanoushadha should he given in case of inadequate virechan or kapha pitta dominance. Peya aggravates kapha dosha. Hence instead of peya, mantha or yusha should be given and instead of vilepi, ghana tarpana (ghana-thick) may be given.

c. Parihaarya Vishay : The don'ts are as follows :

Don'ts (Pariharya Vishay)

a. Speaking aloud

b. Over eating

c. Standing for a long period

d. Resorting anger and grief

e. Exposure to sun, stormy winds

f. Travelling by vehicles

g. Indulging in sexual intercourse

h. Suppression of natural urges like passing of urine, stools etc.

i. Sleeping during day time.

j. Vigil during the night

k. Intake of heavy diet.

Indications for Virechan :

1. Jwara (fever)
2. Kushtha (skin disease)
3. Prameha (Diabetes)
4. Urdhwaga rakta pitta (haemorrhage from external orifices in the upper region of body without external injury)
5. Bhagandar (fistula in ano)
6. Arsha (haemorrhoids)
7. Pleeha vriddhi (spleen enlargement)
8. Gulma (Tumour)
9. Galaganda (inflammation of salivary glands)
10. Granthi (glandular enlargement)
11. Garavish (toxicosis)
12. Vishoochika (gastroenteritis)
13. Alasaka (type of indigestion)
14. Mootraghat (renal failure)
15. Krimi-koshtha (worms)
16. Visarpa (erysipelas)
17. Paandu (anaemia)
18. Shirashoola (headache)
19. Paarshwa shoola (pain in sides of chest)
20. Udaavarta
21. Netradaah (burning sensation in eyes)
22. Aasyadaha (burning sensation in mouth/stomatitis)
23. Hridroga (heart disease)

24. Vyanga (fleshy mole)
25. Neelika (bluish black mole)
26. Aruchi (anorexia)
27. Netra sraava (exudation from eyes)
28. Nasa sraava (exudation from nose)
29. Haleemaka (type of jaundice)
30. Shwaasa (dyspnoea/asthma)
31. Kaasa (cough)
32. Apachi
33. Apasmara (epilepsy)
34. Unmaada (insanity)
35. Vaata rakta (gout)
36. Yonidosha (gynaec disorder)
37. Reto dosha (seminal disorder)
38. Timira (opthalmic disorder)
39. Udara (Ascitis)
40. Avipaak (indigestion)
41. Chhardi (Vomiting)
42. Visphota (eruption)
43. Pakvashay ruja (Pain in large gut)
44. Vibandha (constipation)
45. Vidradhi (abscess)
46. Shvayathu (oedema)
47. Agnidagdha (burns caused by fire)

48. Kshara dagdha (burns caused by alkalies)
49. Shastra kshata (injury caused by instrument/weapon)
50. Dushta vranas (chronic ulcers)
51. Akshipaaka (inflammation of eyes)
52. Abhishyand (conjunctivitis)
53. Kaacha (disease of eye)
54. Gudadaaha (burning sensation in anus)
55. Medhra daaha (burning sensation in penis)
56. Nasa daaha (burning sensation in nose)
57. Karna daaha (burning sensation in ear)
58. Anaaha (distention of abdomen)
59. Shleepada (Elephentiasis)
60. Stanya dosha (vitiation of breast milk)
61. Hrillasa (nausea) etc.

Contraindication for Virechan :

1. Subhaga (delicate)
2. Kshata guda (ulceration of rectum/anus)
3. Muktanaala (rectal prolapse)
4. Adhoga rakta pitta (bleeding from external orifices in lower region)
5. Langhita (fasting)
6. Alpaagni (less digestion power)
7. Niroodha (who have taken evacuative enema)
8. Kamavyagra (agitated by passion)

9. Ajeerna (afflicted with indigestion)
10. Navajwara (acute fever)
11. Madaatyaya (alcoholism)
12. Vaatadhmaan (distension of abdomen)
13. Shalyardita (foreign body)
14. Abhighaata (injury)
15. Atisnigdha (over unctousness)
16. Atirooksha (over dryness)
17. Daaroon Koshtha
18. Kshata ksheena (weakness due to any injury)
19. Atisthoola (too much obesity)
20. Ati krusha (emaciated)
21. Baala (children)
22. Vriddha (old aged people)
23. Durbala (weak)
24. Pipaasita (thirsty)
25. Karmabhaara (over exertion)
26. Upavaasita (fasting)
27. Maithuna prasakta (excessive indulgence in sex)
28. Adhyayana prasakta (exertion due to excessive studies)
29. Vyayaama prasakta (excessive exercise)
30. Chinta prasakta (mental stress)
31. Garbhini (pregnant women)
32. Navapratishyaaya (acute coryza)

33. Raajayakshma (Tubeculosis)

34. Kshudhita (hungry)

35. Nityadukhita (always in sad mood)

36. Hridroga (cardiac disorders)

37. Bhaya-bheeta (Fearful)

❖❖❖

6

BASTI

6. Basti

Instruments Used

The basic instruments necessary for administration of basti are :

- Basti netra
- Basti putaka

Basti netra is a kind of tube which is to be introduced inside the body through anus. This bastinetra is made from either gold, silver, copper etc. The bastinetra is hollow with one end having lumen approximately equal to the thumb and the other end having lumen approximately equal to the little finger. The length of the bastinetra is decided according to the age, as follows:

Age of the patient	Length of bastinetra
1-6 years	6 Angul
7 year	$6^{1/3}$ Angul
8 year	$6^{2/3}$ Angul
9 year	7 Angual
10 years	$7^{1/3}$ Angul
11 years	$7^{2/3}$ Angul
12 years	8 Angul
13 years	$8^{1/2}$ Angul
14 years	9 Angul
15 years	$9^{1/2}$ Angul
16 years	10 Angul
17 years	$10^{1/2}$ Angul

18 years	11 Angul
19 years	$11^{1/2}$ Angul
20 years	12 Angul
Above 20 years	12 Angul
Angula is the breadth of the finger of that patient.	

Bastinetra has three ridges on it. The first one is on the $1/4^{th}$ part of basti netra near the narrow end. This first ridge prevents the entry of bastinetra above this level. The other two ridges are at the other end, of which one is at 2 angula from the broader end and the other at the same end. Bastinetra of uttar basti is also called as pushpanetra. This should be of gold or silver. This bastinetra has only two ridges. The size of lumen of bastinetra is equal to the size of a mustard seed.Basti putak: This is the reservior of basti material during administration of basti. Basti putak is tied to basti netra with the help of a string. The urinary bladder of animals like buffalo, bull, deer etc is taken for this purpose. This bladder is then cleaned, dried and oleated to maintain its elasticity. The bladder should be free from foul smells; the size should not be very big; it should not be very muscular or thick. The basti putak (bladder) is then tied to the basti netra tightly with the help of a string to avoid leakage.

Nirooha Basti

Indications:

Vata sanga (obstruction of vata)

Mootra sanga (obstruction of urine)

Mala sanga (constipation)

Shukra sanga (obstrution of semen)

Bala kshaya (loss of strength)

Mansa kshaya (loss of muscle tissue)

Shukra kshaya (Excess loss of semen)

Adhman (Abdominal distention due to flatulence)

Krumikoshtha (worm infestation)

Parvabheda (pain in joints)

Bhagandara (fistula in ano)

Pleeha dosha (diseases of spleen)

Unmada (insanity)

Hritshoola (angina pectoris)

Parshwa shoola (pain in sides of chest)

Prushtha shoola (backache)

Aakshepaka (convulsions)

Raja kshaya (amenorrhoea)

Vishamagni (impaired appetite)

Sandhigata vata (osteo arthritis)

Arsha (haemorrhoids)

Shosha (emaciation)

Stambha (stiffness)

Vatavyadhi (disorders of vatadosha)

Ardita (facial palsy)

Pakshaghata (Paraplegia)

Upadansha (gonorrhoea)

Vatarakta (gout)

Stanyashosha (lack of breast milk)

Mutrakruchhra (burning micturation/urinary tract infections)

Mootrashmari (urinary calculii)

Contra indications

Sr. No.	Contra indications	Complications if basti administered,where it is contraindicated.
1.	Ajeerna (indigestion)	Dushyodar (a kind of ascitis), shotha (oedema), murchha (unconsciousness)
2.	Atisnigdha (unctuousness in excess)	Dushyodar (a kind of ascitis),shotha (oedema), murchha (unconsciousness)
3.	Peetasneha (who has consumed unctous material)	Dushyodar (a kind of ascitis), shotha (oedema), murchha (unconsciousness)
4.	Atidurbala (weak individuals)	Dyspnoea
5.	Atikrusha (very thin)	Becomes more kruśha (thin)
6.	Kshudharta (hungry)	Dyspnoea
7.	Trushnarta (thirsty)	Dyspnoea
8.	After nasya	Srotorodha (obstruc-ion in srotas)
9.	After vaman, virechan	Irritation of GI tract and dryness in the body increases.

10.	Kruddha (enraged), fearful	Basti material goes above the level of pakwashaya.
11.	Moorchhita (unconsciousness)	Hridayopaghata (cardiac failure)
12.	Chhardi(afflicted with vomiting)	Aggravation of disease
13.	Prasakta nisthiva	Aggravation of disease
14.	Baddhagudodar (intestinal obstruction)	severe flatulence and death
15.	Prameha (diabetes)	Aggravation of disease if not given according to the conditioh of doshas.

Poorvakarma

Pradhan karma (Main operative) of administration of nirooha basti is a simple procedure. Howerver during poorvakarma one should be very careful. Main points that should be taken into consideration before administering the basti are as follows:

Dosha : Basti is the best treatment for vata disorders. However with few changes in the medicines, the basti can be given for pitta and kapha disorders. The sites where doshas are vitiated and state of vitiated doshas should,be considered properly. If the vitiated doshas are in aamashay (stomach) vaman should be administered. And if doshas are in pakwashay (intestine), virechan or basti should be administered.

According to vitiated dosha the number of basti is decided.

For kapha/kapha predominant diseases 1-3 basties are given In pitta / pitta predominant diseases 5-7 basties are given, and in vata/vata predominant disorders 9-11 basties are given.

Dose : Dose of Nirooha for one year old child is 1/2 prasruti. Later, 1/2 prasruti should be increased yearly. The same hike is maintained upto 12 years of age. Then for next each year 1. prasruti should be increased yearly. This hike is maintained up to 18 years of age. This particular dose of 960 gm. is maintained upto 70 years of age. After that the dose is 800 gm. i.e., same as for 16 years of age. One prasruti is 8 tolas, which is around 80 gms.

Age	Dose	Grams
1	1/2 Prasruti	40 gm.
2	1 Prasruti	80 gm.
3	1 1/2 Prasruti	120 gm.
4	2 prasruti	160 gm.
5	2 1/2 Prasruti	200 gm.
6	3 Prasruti	240 gm.
7	3 1/2 Prasruti	280 gm.
8	4 Prasruti	320 gm.
9	4 1/2 Prasruti	360 gm.
10	5 Prasruti	400 gm.
11	5 1/2 Prasruti	440 gm.
12	6 Prasruti	480 gm.
13	7 Prasruti	560 gm.
14	8 Prasruti	640 gm.
15	9 Prasruti	720 gm.

16	10 Prasruti	800 gm.
17	11 Prasruti	880 gm.
18	12 Prasruti	960 gm.
19-70	12 Prasruti	960 gm.
Above 70	10 Prasruti	800 gm.

In basti medicine of Nirooha, some amount of unctuous material is to be added (commonly ghee/oil). In vata predominant diseases 1/4 th of the decoction, in pitta predominant diseases and in healthy persons 1/6th of the decoction and in kapha predominant disease 1/8 th of the decoction, sneh (unctuous material) is added. Basti material should neither be too hot nor too cold. Very cold basti material causes vitiation of vata dosha in the body-giving rise to flatulence, constipation etc. However very hot basti material causes vitiation of pitta-giving rise to diarrhoea, giddiness etc.

Kaal (time and season): Kaal can be taken according to the season as well as the timings of the day. The right season for basti in a person is 'Varsha rutu' i.e., monsoon season. In 'varsha rutu' vata dosha is in prakopavastha (provoked state). In case of a individual undergoing all the five karmas, virechan is given 15 days after vaman and nirooha is given 7 days after virechan.

Aatur siddhata (preparation of the patient): The patient is first oleated externally and fomented. Internal oleation is contraindicated. If the body of the patient is very an unctous, 2-3 anuvasan basties are to be given to alleviate vata dosha and after that Nirooha Basti is administered.

Medicines used and Preparation of Basti Material : Honey, saindhav (rock salt), unctous material, kalka (paste of herbs), decoction of herbs are taken in the same sequence as the basic ingredients for a nirooha basti. Generally for vata/vata predominant disorders and even for healthy people decoction of dashamoola can be used as basti material. Basti netra (nozzle) is chosen according to the age of the patient. Basti putak (urinary bladder taken out from an animal) is filled with the basti material and then is tied with the basti netra. For convenience the enema pot with a rubber tube and a catheter is usually used now a days instead of a bladder.

Pradhan Karma

The patient is advised to lie down in the left lateral position (vaamaparshwa) as the guda (rectum), pakwashay (large intestine) and grahani are on the same side. The left leg is kept straight. The right leg is flexed in hip joint and knee joint and brought close to the abdomen. The left arm is kept below the head. The anus is lubricated with oil or ghee and then basti netra is slowly inserted inside the anal canal. Now the basti putak is squeezed gently till basti putak is evacuated in such a way that little quantity of basti material remains inside.

If the enema pot is used, a catheter is inserted upto $4^{1/2}$-$6^{1/2}$ inches inside the anus. The pot is given some elevation so as to enhance the flow of material and hence basti is adminstered. Then the basti netra is taken out. The patient is advised to lie down in the same position for a couple of minutes. During the administration of basti the patient is asked to breathe deeply.

Pratyagama of basti : The evacuation of basti material from the body is called 'basti pratyagama'. The time for pratyagam is a maximum of 48 minutes (one muhurta). If basti doesn't come out within 48 minutes, strong nirooha basti is given. i.e., yavakshar, cow's urine, trikatu (Piper longum, Piper nigrum and Zinzeber officinalis) etc. Phalavarti (Ayurvedic suppositories) can also be used for the same purpose.

Signs and symptoms of proper/improper basti :

Optimum effects (proper basti) :

- Stools, vitiated pitta, vitiated kapha and vitiated vata are eliminated respectively.
- Feeling of lightness in the body.
- Agni (digestive capacity) is increased.
- The symptoms of the disease are relieved gradually.
- The strength increases gradually.

Improper Effects :

Ayoga : If the nirooha basti is not given properly or doesn't work properly it gives following symptoms:Pain in head, cardiac region, umbilicus, rectum, penis; oedema (shotha), coryza (pratishyay), nausea, dyspnoea, heaviness in the body etc.

Atiyoga : In atiyoga following symptoms are seen:

Tremors, giddiness, weakness, episodes of black outs, hiccoup etc.

Pashchat karma :

Pathya (Dietetic & behavioural regimen) : After the elimination of basti material, the patient is advised to take rest. Then after sometime the patient is advised to bathe with lukewarm water. According to the agni and status of doshas, the meal containing milk, yusha, mansarasa (meat-soup) is given. But the diet should be 1/3rd of the usual diet. And in the evening anuvasan basti is adminstered.

The dietetic regimen should be followed for twice the number of days of basti course.

Anuvasan Basti

Indications: All those diseases indicated for nirooha are also indicated for anuvasan basti. Moreover those individuals with very ununctous body, whose digestive power is very strong and in whom vata dosha is in provoked state are also indicated for anuvasan basti.

Contra indications:

S.N.	Contraindications	Complications if anuvasan basti is administered when contraindicated
1.	Abhuktabhakta (without ingestion of food)	Aadhmana (flatulence) Chhardi (vomiting) etc.
2.	Navajwara (Acute fever)	Udara (ascitis)
3.	Kamala (jaundice)	Udara (ascitis)
4.	Pandu (anaemia)	Udara (ascitis)
5.	Prameha (diabetes)	Udara (ascitis)
6.	Arsha (haemorrhoids)	Aadhmana (flatulence)
7.	Arochaka	Aggravation of disease
8.	Agnimandya (suppression of digestive power)	Agnimandya increases
9.	Durbala (weak)	Agnimandya increases
10.	Pratishyaya (coryza)	Aggravation of disease
11.	Plehavruddhi (splenomegaly)	Aggravation of disease

12.	Krumi koshtha (worm infestation)	Worms move upwards towards aamashaya
13.	Aadhya vata (gout)	Aggravation of disease
14.	Sthaulya (obesity)	Obesity increases
15.	Atisara (diarrhoea)	Aggravation of disease

Poorvakarma

Aatur Siddhata (preparation of the patient)

The patient is first oleated (external oleation) and fomented.

- Ingestion of food: The patient is advised to have a light meal. Presence of food in aamashay prevents the entry of sneha from anuvasan basti in aamashaya. Hence the sneha remains in pakwashaya where it's action is expected. The food should not be very unctuous or very ununctuous. The quantity of food should be 14th the quantity of normal diet.
- Chankramanadi (strolling): After ingestion of food the person is advised to stroll around for a distance of about 100 yards (chankraman). Then the patient is advised to pass urine and stool.

Medicines used and preparation of basti material :

Generally sneha (according to the disease) with saindhav (rock salt) and shatavha is used. This material is warmed in hot water bath. According to the quantity, the basti containing sneha is of 3 types.

- Sneha basti - 6 'pal' = 240 gm (approx.)
- Anuvasan basti - 3 'pal' = 120 gm (approx.)
- Matra basti - $1^{1/2}$ 'pal' = 60 gm (approx.)

Matra basti is recommended for weak persons, children, aged persons etc.

Kaal Vichar (Time of administration)

In cold climate, in shishir (late winter) and hemant (early winter) season, anuvasan should be administered in day time in sharad (autum), grishma (summer) and varsha (monsoon) seasons anuvasna should be administered in the night. Similarly, in weak patients, in very unuctous patients, in the patients suffering from vata disorders, anuvasan basti can be given in the night. Here meaning of night is just after the evening hours.

Pradhan Karma

The same position, as in administration of nirooha basti is given to the patient. The anus is lubricated and the bastinetra or the catheter is inserted slowly inside the anus and the basti putak is squeezed gently to evacuate the basti putak. After administration of basti the patient is advised to remain in the same position for a couple of minutes. During administration of basti the patient is asked to breathe deeply.

Basti Pratyagam : The evacuation of basti material from the body is called 'basti pratyagam' The expected time period for basti pratyagam is 12 hours i.e., the basti material should come out of the body within 12 hours. If basti material does not come out even after 24 hours and if the patient is asymptomatic, then there is no necessity to carry out any procedures. But in case the patient shows some symptoms like pain in abdomen etc., then proper procedures like phalavarti (Ayurvedic suppositary) etc. should be carried out for basti pratyagama.

Pashchat Karma

Dietetic Regimen : After anuvasan basti, patient is asked to rest for a while. Lukewarm water medicated with shunthi (Zinziber officinale) and dhaniya (Coriander sativus) is given to the patient. This water with shunthi and dhaniya helps in digestion of sneha. Light, warm food is given to the patient when he feels hungry.

Uttar Basti

Indications

- Indications for uttar basti given in urinary bladder - 13 kinds of mutrakruchhra (urinary disorders), infertility in men, seminal disorders.
- Indications for uttar basti given in uterus :

1. Yonibhransha (uterine prolapse).
2. Pain in vagina and uterus.
3. Rajodosha (menorrhagia, amenorrhoea, dysmenorrhoea etc.)
4. Infertility
5. Yonivyapad (20 kinds of disorders of vagina and uterus).

Poorvakarma

Aatur siddhata (preparation of the patient): Uttar basti recommended for uterine disorders, is to be given in rutukal. Rutukal is the period of 16 days starting from the first day of menstruration.

The patient is first oleated (external oleation) and fomented. Yavagu with milk and ghee or food containing meat soup should be given prior to uttar basti.

Medicines used and preparation of basti material : Sneha (unctuous material) or freshly prepared kwath (decoction) should be used. This should be luke warm. For relieving pain, decoction of pippali can be used. In menorrhagia decoction of Ashoka (Saraca asoca), Lodhra (Symplocaos racemosa) can be used.

Pradhankarma

In case of male patient, the patient is asked to sit on a wooden table. The penis is oleated and then the bastinetra is inserted through urethra. The medicine is pushed gently inside the bladder.

Observation

If kwath is administered, it will come out very quickly. If sneha is administered it will remain in the body for a longer duration. In case of uttar basti in uterus, sneha comes out quickly. Uttar basti can be given at an interval of three days.

Pashchatkarma

If basti does not come out within 12 hours, phalavarti (Ayurvedic suppositories) can be administered, e.g., pippalyadi varti, aragwadhadi varti. This varti is administered in anus by which apan (type of vata) gets stimulated and brings the basti out of the body.

Dietetic Regimen

After basti pratyagam, food-containing milk, yusha or meat soup should be given.

Sub Types

1. **Yapan Basti :** This is a kind of basti specifially used to increase the strength of mansa dhatu and shukra dhatu, qualitatively and quantitatively. This basti increases the life span of a subject. In this basti, kwath either with milk, meat soup, honey, ghee, jaggery, eggs etc. are used. Charakacharya has recommended 26 such basties for enhancement of health.

2. **Prasrut Yogiki Basti :** Generally the quantity of basti material is decided according to the age. But there are few basties in which the quantity is same for all age groups.

Those basties in which quantity is one prasrut, approximately, equal to 80 g is called ' prasrut yogiki basti'.

3. **Dwadash Prasrụtiki Basti** : In this basti the quantity is 12 prasruti (960 gm. Approximately). The example of this type is Madhutailik basti:

   Honey is 2 prasrut = 160 gm.

   Sneha is 3 prasrut = 240 gm.

   Kalka (paste of herbs) is 1 prasrut = 80 gm.

   Kwath (decoction) is 4 prasrut = 320 gm.

   Powdered medicines & saindhav (rock salt) is 2 prasrut = 160 gm.

   Thus in all, total is 12 prasrut = 960 gm.

4. **Padaheen basti :** The total quantity in this basti is 9 prasrut = 720 gm approximately.

5. **Teekshna basti :** Basti containing kshar, urine and ushna (hot), teekshna (penetrating) medicines, is called teekshna basti. This basti is used when the Nirooha basti doesn't come out within 48 minutes.

6. **Pichha basti :** This contains the medicines of pichhil property. This basti is used in Pravahika (dysentry and ulcerative colitis).

7. **Rakta basti :** In case of Pandu (anaemia), basti of blood of animals is given. This basti is called Rakta basti.

7.

NASYA

7. Nasya

Introduction

Nasya is a procedure in which the medicines are administered through nasal route.

Nose is the approach to the interior of the head; so it is considered to be effective in diseases of head & also the controlling centres of five sense organs (Indriyas) as they are situated in head region. In this procedure, vitiaed doshas above sternal notch i.e. in the head and neck, are either eliminated or pacified. In other words, substances administered by this route pervade the head and destroy the disorders in this part of the body. For this procedure, the medicines used are - oil, pastes, powders, plant juices, decoctions, infusions and medicinal fumes.

Types

General

Types of Nasya can be divided

I) **According to action**

1. Shodhan or virechana (Elimination) - For elimination of doshas.
2. Shaman (Pacification) - For pacification of doshas.
3. Brunhan (Tonification) - For subsidence of vata.

II) **According to the substances used :**

1. Avapeeda - Juice Squeezed from fresh herbs is used.
2. Navana - Liquids like milk & oils are used.
3. Dhooma - Fumes of various dry herbs are used.
4. Dhmapana - Medicinal powders are used.

III) According to the dose :

1. Pratimarsha - A dose of 2 drops in each nostril.
2. Marsha - 8 to 32 drops in each nostril.

Main types of Nasya

1. Navan	2. Avapeeda	3. Dhmapan
4. Dhoom	5. Marsha	6. Shiro Virechana

Some other types considered in the text

Tarpan - Nourishing

Karshana - Depleting

Sneha - Nasya done with the sneha dravyas (substance) i.e., oil, ghee etc.

Prayogika - Frequent

Stambhana - To cease the bleeding from the nose in case of epistaxis

CONTRAINDICATION	Complication caused due to administration of Nasya when contraindicated
Ajeerna (indigestion), just after intake of food.	May cause cough, dyspnoea, vomiting
Just after intake of sneha afflicted with thirst	May produce discharge from mouth
Shirasnanottara (After head bath or when desiring to take head bath)	May cause coryza
Kshudhit (Afflicted with hunger)	May cause increased thirst, dryness of mouth

Abhighat (External injury)	May aggravate the pain
Exhaustion due to coitus, physical exercise or drinking	May cause pain in the head shoulder, eye & chest
Jwarita (Acute fever), Dukkhi (Grief stricken).	May aggravate fever or may cause defects of vision
Anuvasita (After Anuvasan basti)	May cause heaviness in the head
Garbhini (Pregnant lady)	May affect the health of the foetus.
Unsuitable season, bad weather	May cause diseases like cough, coryza etc. and head diseases (Head-ache due to various reasons)

Navan

This type of Nasya can be used daily. Liquids like milk and oils are used. This is of two types :

1. Shodhana - (Purification)
2. Snehana - (Oleation)

This type of Nasya gives strength to neck, shoulder and chest region. It is also used to improve eye sight.

Navan Nasya is used to cure some diseases like Vataja Shiroroga, Karnashoola (Earache), Karna Kshweda (Tinnitus), Avabahuka (Frozen shoulder etc.)

Avapeeda

Juice of fresh herbs is used. According to Charakacharya, there are two types of avapeeda Nasya -

1. Shodhan
2. Stambhana

According to Sushrut; Avapeeda is a kind of shodhan or

virechana nasya.

Dhmapan or Pradhaman

This is a variety of shodhan nasya. The medicinal powder is blown into the nose by a special apparatus. This Nasya is indicated in pratishyay (rhinitis) and in mental disorders like epilepsy, insanity, etc.

Dhooma

Dhooma nasya is inhalation of fumes produced by burning various herbs. This nasya is classified into three varieties -

1. Sneha 2. Virechan 3. Shamana

Marsha

The Sneha or unctuous material is used in this type of nasya.

Marsha dose is 8-32 drops in each nostril. Pratimarsha 2 drops in each nostril.

Complications are very rare in the use of pratimarsha nasya.

Pratimarsha nasya can be administered in all seasons of the year.

According to Vagbhata Pratimarsha Nasya is to be used fourteen times in a day.

Shirovirechana

This is a kind of nasya which eliminates the doshas.

Medicated powders or strong oils are used in this type of Nasya.

Indications - Disorders of eye, ear, nose, throat -

- Headache including migraine (Shiroroga)
- Manyastambha (stiffness in head, neck, shoulders)
- Dantashoola (Toothache), Loosening of the teeth

- Netrashoola (Eye pain), Disturbed vision, disorders of cornea and eyelids.
- Peenas (Sinusitis)
- Nasashoola (Nasal pain)
- Aardita (Facial paralysis)
- Apasmar (Epilepsy)
- Nidranasha (Insomnia)
- Unmad (Insanity)
- Vakdosha (Hoarseness of voice, obstructed speech, stammering & loss of speech)

Poorva karma

The patient is advised to empty the bladder and bowels.

A light meal is advised if the patient is hungry.

1. **Snehan :** Application of oil is done on head, face, forehead, shoulder and nasal region.
2. **Swedan :** Mild fomentation should be done with the help of a cloth.
3. Instruments used -

According to type of Nasya -

1. Navan or Marsha - Dropper
2. Dhmapan - Special apparatus of rubber or a rubber tube or paper tube.
3. Dhooma - Dhoomayantra

Medicines used -

A. Herbs

1. Apamarga seeds - Achyranthus aspera

2. Pippali - Piper longum
3. Marich - Piper nigrum
4. Shunthi - Zinziber officinale
5. Vidang - Embelia ribes
6. Tulsi - Ocimum sanctum
7. Haridra - Curcuma longa
8. Brahmi - Centella asiatica
9. Madanaphala - Randia dumatorum
10. Devdaru - Cedrus deodara
11. Trikatu - Mixture of shunthi, marich and pippali

B. Oils - Sesame oil

C. Medicated oils - Anu oil, Vacha oil, Padmakadi oil, Panchendriyavardhana oil, Shadbindu oil, Jatyadi oil, Nirgundi oil, etc.

D. Ghruta (Ghee) - Cow ghee, Shatavari Ghruta, Brahmi - Ghruta, etc.

E. Other - Milk, Honey

3. Timing of Nasya -

A. For a healthy person, nasya should be given in mid day.

B. According to season -

a) Summer - In between 6 a.m. to 11 a.m.

b) Winter - In the afternoon between 12 to 2 p.m.

c) Rainy - When the weather is not cloudy.

Pradhankarma

1. The patient is advised to lie down on the back with his head tilted slightly backwards.
2. The medicine is administered in each nostril separately. The patient is advised to breathe deeply.

Paschat Karma

After nasya, mild fomentation is done on forehead, face, throat & neck. Soft massage is done on the back of the neck, shoulder region and feet. Kawal and Dhoomapan is advised after this. Then the patient is advised to rest for a while after taking light food with lukewarm water.

Regimen to be followed -

1. After nasya; cold water is contraindicated for drinking or any other purpose.
2. Exposure to dust, wind and excessive walking should be avoided immediately after nasya.

I) Signs of proper and improper nasya -

i) Proper - Feeling of lightness in head and body, good sleep, proper functioning of sense organs & mind, elimination of vitiated doshas from nasal sinuses & nose, relief from signs and symptoms of disease.

ii) Improper or Inadequate Nasya - Signs of vata aggravation like dryness in the nose with itching. In this case; again proper nasya medicine is administered in the nose.

iii) Improper - Excessive purification - There are excessive secretions not only from nose, but also from eyes with severe burning. There might be bleeding from the nose. In such cases; few drops of ghee are instilled in the nose.

Benefits of Nasya -

1. Regular use prevents diseases of ear, nose, throat & head.
2. Very effective for treating diseases like hair fall, baldness. Regular use of nasya can improve the quality of hair.
3. The medicine given by Nasya is absorbed like Intra venous medicine which is fast.
4. The Bioavailability of medicine given by Nasya is more than that taken through mouth.

Nasya controls all doshas in the region of head & all centers situated in the head. It is useful in the treatment of various diseases like headache, migraine, facial paralysis, hemiplegia, etc.

8.
RAKTAMOKSHANA

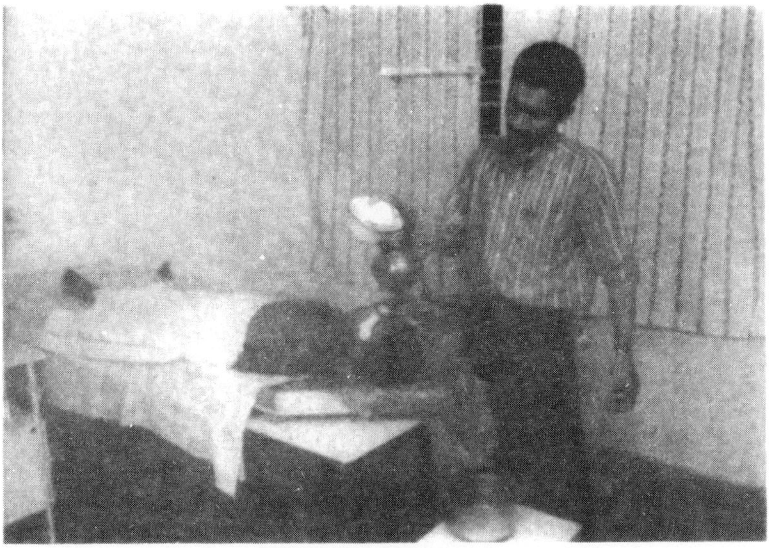

Shirodhara

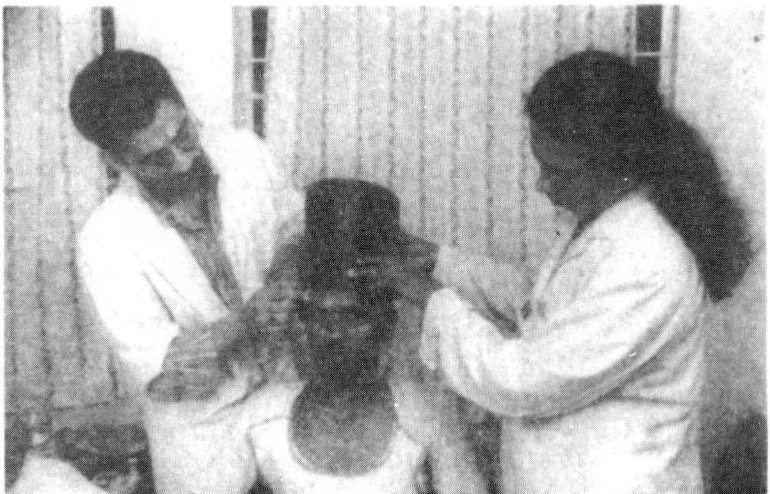

Shirobasti

Swedan

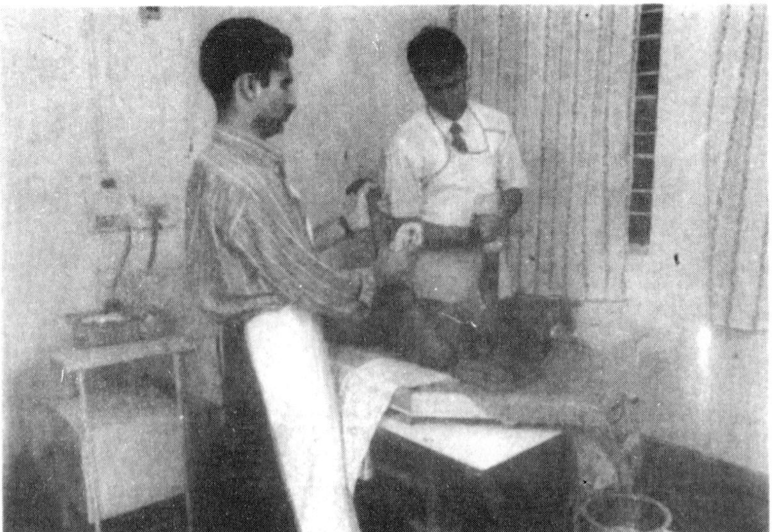

Pindaswed

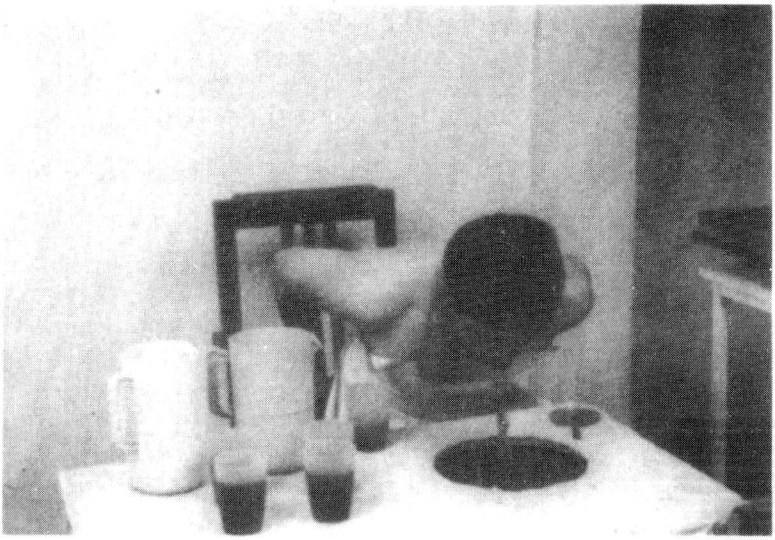

Vaman

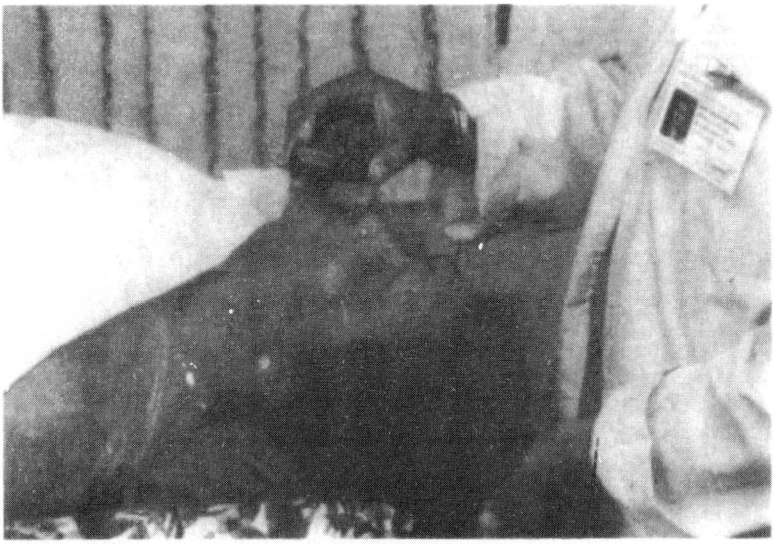

Nasya

Dahanakarma

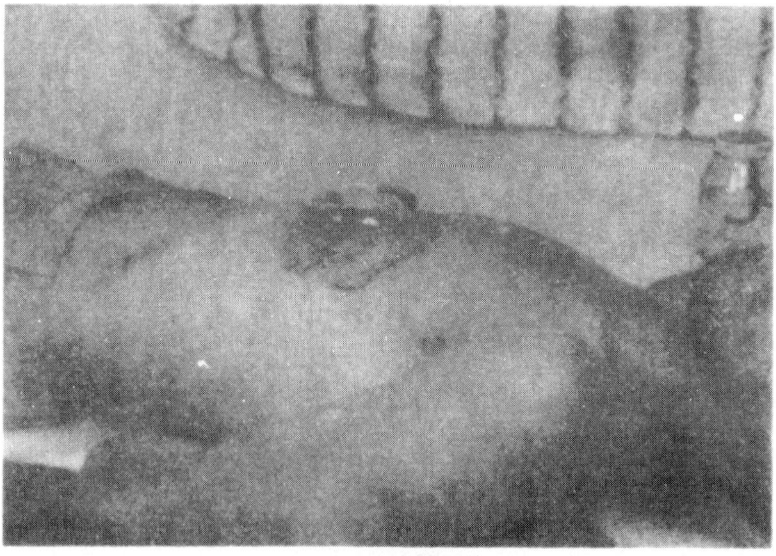

Hrudbasti

8. Raktamokshana

Introduction

The procedure of blood letting from the body is known as Raktamokshana

Aims & Objective :

Rakta is an important dhatu, which performs the function of jeevan (life) in the body. But after vitiation; it causes many diseases, which are known as raktaja Rogas. Due to this property, it has also been named as the fourth dosha in some Ayurvedic texts.

Rakta is an important site of pitta. Raktamokshana is the best therapy and is done for managing the diseases caused by rakta and pitta. Raktamokshana is an important therapeutic part in Shalya Tantra i.e., Ayurvedic Branch.

Types : Jalauka

Jalkaukavacharn

Jalauka Shodhana

Before use Jalaukas are purified with water mixed with turmeric i.e., Carcuma longa. They are kept in this water for 48 minutes; to activate them for best result.

Pradhankarma

Application : The patient is advised to lie down and the part of the body on which the jalauka is to be applied is rubbed with powdered cow-dung and soil without causing pain. To fix it quickly, apply a drop of milk or blood at the part of the body to which the jalauka is to be applied. Then it starts sucking the blood. The body of jalauka is covered with a piece of wet cotton. When the jalauka has sucked sufficient quantity of blood, it gets detached by itself or it is removed by applying turmeric powder at the mouth of the jalauka.

Now some turmeric powder should be applied to the mouth of jalauka and it should be squeezed lightly towards the mouth end, until the blood is vomited. Once vomited it should be kept in fresh water. This jalauka should not be used for next 7 days. The dressing at the site is done with honey or cold water or turmeric powder or shatadhaut ghruta.

Indication :

Sr. No.	Disease	Charaka	Sushruta	Vagabhata
1.	Kushtha (skin disease)	+	+	+
2.	Visarpa (erysipelas)	+	+	+
3.	Pidika (eruption)	+	+	+
4.	Raktapitta	+	+	-
5.	Asrigdara (menorrhagia)			
6.	Gudapaka (inflammation of anus / rectum)	+		-
7.	Medhrapaka (inflammation of penis)	+	+	-
8.	Mukhapaka (stomatitis)	+	+	-
9.	Pleeha (disorders of spleen)	+	+	+
10.	Gulma	+	+	+

11.	Vidradhi (abscess)	+	+	+
12.	Neelika (blue moles)	+	+	-
13.	Vyanga (freckles)	+	+	+
14.	Piplu	+	-	+
15.	Dadru (a kind of skin disease)	+	-	-
16.	Tilakalaka (black moles)	+	+	-
17.	Shvitra (leucoderma)	+	-	-
18.	Pama (scabies)	+	-	-
19.	Upa kusha (pyorrhoea alveolar)	+	-	+
20.	Prameelaka	+	-	-
21.	Vatarakta (gout)	+	-	+
22.	Vaivarnya (discoloration)	+	+	-
23.	Agnimandya (suppression of digestive capacity)	+	-	+
24.	{Pipasa (thirst)	+	+	+
25.	Kandu (pruritis)	+	+	-
26.	Kotha (tissue decomposition)	+	-	-
27.	Mashaka	+	-	-
28.	Nyacha	-	+	-
29.	Indralupta (alopecia areata)	- -	 +	- -

30.	Arsha (haemorrhoids)	-	+	-
+ : Indicated by the author. - : Not indicated by the author.				

Contraindications :

1. Sarvangashotha (oedema all over the body)
2. Durbala (weak)
3. Pandu (anaemia)
4. Arsha (haemorrhoids)
5. Udara-shoola (pain in abdomen)
6. Grahani (irritable bowel syndrome)
7. Kamala (jaundice)
8. Vriddha (old aged person)
9. Rukshashareera (excessive dryness in the body)
10. Kshata-Ksheena
11. Shranta (tired)
12. Madyasakta (alcoholism)
13. Vamita (just after vaman)
14. Asthapita (just after nirooha basti)
15. Anuvasita (just after anuvasan basti)
16. Klaibya (infertility / impotence)
17. Kasa (cough)
18. Shwasa (dyspnoea/asthma)

19. Shosha (emaciation)
20. Pyrexia (fever)
21. Akshipaka (inflammation of eyes)
22. Pakshaghata (palsy)
23. Upavasita (person undergoing langhan i.e. fast)
24. Pipasita (thirsty)
25. Moorchhita (unconscious) etc.

Procedure

Period for Raktamokshana :

Seasons (ritu) :

1. Sharad ritu (Autumn season) Day on which climate is not cloudy and its neither too hot nor too cold.
2. Varsha ritu (rainy season) On the day which is free from cloud.
3. Greeshma ritu (summer season) in morning or evening time.
4. Hemant ritu : Midday

Siravyadha

Venesection :- In this procedure the blood is made to ooze out from a vein. Siravyadha is done with a sharp instrument and is a more severe form of blood-letting than the application of leeches. The vein selection depends on the diseased part of the body. The lancet is inserted gently neither too deep nor superficial in the vein.

The maximum quantity of blood that may be let out should not exceed one prastha i.e., 640 gms. at a time. The operated site should be bandaged with a piece of cloth soaked in medicated oil. Sushruta states that cold water should be applied to stop the bleeding and then astringent decoction or medicated ash o (kshara) should be applied.

Sr. No.	Disease	Charaka	Sushruta	Vagabhata
1.	Kustha (skin disease)	+	+	+
2.	Visarpa (erysepalas)	+	+	+
3.	Pidika (eruption)	+	+	+
4.	Raktapitta	+	+	-
5.	Asrigdara (menorrhagia)	+	+	-
6.	Gudapaka (inflammation of anus / rectum)	+	+	-
7.	Medhrapaka (inflammation of penis)	+	+	-
8.	Mukhapaka (stomatitis)	+	+	-
9.	Pleeha (disorders of spleen)	+	+	+
10.	Gulma	+	+	+
11.	Vidradhi (abscess)	+	+	+
12.	Neelika (blue moles)	+	+	-

13.	Vyanga (freckles)	+	+	+
14.	Piplu	+	-	+
15.	Dadru (a kind of skin disease)	+	-	-
16.	Tilakalaka (black moles)	+	+	-
17.	Shvitra (leucoderma)	+	-	-
18.	Pama (scabies)	+	-	-
19.	Upa kusha (pyorrhoea alveolar)	+	-	+
20.	Prameelaka	+	-	-
21.	Vatarakta (gout)	+	-	+
22.	Vaivarnya (discoloration)	+	+	-
23.	Agnimandya (suppression of digestive capacity)	+	-	+
24.	{Pipasa (thirst)	+	+	+
25.	Kandu (pruritis)	+	+	-
26.	Kotha (tissue decomposition)	+	-	-
27.	Mashaka	+	-	-
28.	Nyacha	-	+	-
29.	Indralupta (alopecia areata)	-	+	-
30.	Arsha (haemorrhoids)	-	+	-

+ : Indicated by the author.
- : Not indicated by the author.

Contraindications :

25. Sarvangashotha (oedema all over the body)
26. Durbala (weak)
27. Pandu (anaemia)
28. Arsha (haemorrhoids)
29. Udara-shoola (pain in abdomen)
30. Grahani (irritable bowel syndrome)
31. Kamala (jaundice)
32 Vridha (old aged person)
33. Rukshashareera (excessive dryness in the body)
34. Kshata-Ksheena
35. Shranta (tired)
36. Madyasakta (alcoholism)
37. Vamita (just after vaman)
38. Asthapita (just after nirooha basti)
39. Anuvasita (just after anuvasan basti)
40. Klaibya (infertility / impotence)
41. Kasa (cough)
42. Shwasa (dyspnoea/asthama)
43. Shosha (emaciation)
44. Pyrexia (fever)
45. Akshipaka (inflammation of eyes)
46. Pakshaghata (palsy)
47. Upavasita (person undergoing langhan i.e. fast)

48. Pipasita (thirst)

49. Moorchhita (unconscious) etc.

Procedure

Period for Raktamokshana :

Seasons (ritu) :

1. Sharad ritu (Autumn season) Day on which climate is not cloudy and its neither too hot nor too cold.
2. Varsha ritu (rainy season) On the day which is free from cloud.
3. Greeshma ritu (summer season) in morning or evening time.
4. Hemant ritu : Midday

Following points are to be kept in veiw.

1. Doshavastha (status of doshas)
2. Raktavastha (status of raktadhatu)
3. Aaturavastha (condition of the patient)

Prachhan Karma

This is the process by which accumulated or clotted blood is removed with the help of a shastra (instrument).

Joints (sandhi), marma (vital points) are to be excluded from this procedure.

Superficial and parallel cuts are made on the skin very swiftly through which the blood will start oozing out.

This is specially indicated in hyperpigmentation due to clotted blood. This can also be used as a first stage in the procedure of Alabu avacharan and Ghati yantra.

Alabu avacharan

This is a kind of rakta mokshan in which alabu (gourd) is used. Alabu is bitter in taste. It has teekshna (penetrating) and rooksha (dry) properties. Hence it is used in diseases of kapha vitiated blood. An Alabu (gourd) is taken. This should be tender, fresh and of medium size. The front portion is cut open and the gourd is made hollow by removing the contents by using a knife.

A cut is made on the skin at the site of raktamokshana by using a sharp scalpel (prachhan karma). Now the prepared gourd is kept inverted on the cut with a candle inside.

The candle will burn until the air / oxygen inside the gourd gets utilised completely. As the air gets utilised for burning, vacuum created inside will generate negative pressure and the blood will ooze out.

Ghatiyantra

The same principle as in alabu is used in ghatiyantra.

Instead of alabu (gourd) a specially prepared pot can be used.

Shrungavacharan

This is the method of blood letting by using shrung (horn). For this method, usually cows' horns are used as they are hollow inside. This horn is hot in nature, sweet in taste and has an unctous property in it. Hence in case of a disease caused by vata vitiated blood, shrunga is used.

Before using the horn, a cut is made at the site of raktamokshana blood is made to ooze, by using a sharp scalpel (prachhan karma). Now the broader end of the horn which is tied with white, clean cloth is kept on the wound and from the other end or (narrow end) the blood is aspirated.

❖❖❖

9
ALLIED KARMA

9. Allied Karma

Netra Basti

Technique :

Netra basti is a type of local treatment. Retaining the sneha at netra (eye) region is called Netra Basti or Netra Tarpan.

Instruments Used :

Specially prepared eye cap, black gram flour, cow's ghee and water.

Vidhi (procedure) :

A dough of black gram flour of a firm consistency is made. The patient is adviced to lie down in supine position. Specially prepared eye cap is placed over the eye. Dough prepared from black gram flour is used to seal the cap in proper position. It should be sealed properly so that no sneha will leak. Sneha of room temperature is poured in the cap, keeping the eye of patient closed. After this the patient is asked to open and close the eye frequently. After specific time (mentioned below) the sneha is removed by soaking it with the help of cotton. The area is cleaned with cotton. Patient is adviced to avoid bright light immediately after the procedure. According to dosha, time period is as follows :

Vata dosha - 1000 matra = 5.16 minutes approximately

Pitta dosha - 600 matra = 3.18 minutes approximately

Kapha dosha -500 matra = 2.58 minutes approximately

Action : Netra basti nourishes the eye muscles, alleviates the dryness, rigidity and pain in the eye. Eye is the site of Alochak pitta (one of the types of pitta dosha) which plays an important role in performing the normal functions of eye.

Netra basti balances the action of Alochak pitta and vision of eye is improved.

Indications :

Dryness of eyes,

Injury/trauma to the eye,

Restricted movements of eyelids,

Conjunctivitis,

Glaucoma, pthisis bulbi,

Diminished vision,

Supra-orbital Neuralgia,

Muscular weakness of eyes.

Hrid Basti

Technique :

Retaining the sneha at hridaya (cardiac) region on the chest is hrid basti. 'Sneha' is the anitidote for vatadosha. Oil is absorbed in the body through the skin and pacification of vitiated vata dosha is achieved. Hrid basti can be performed in all the diseases of heart. Various oils are used according to the state of vitiated doshas in various diseases. It also gives strength to the cardiac muscles and improves blood circulation.

Instruments used :

The specially prepared ring, black gram flour, water and medicated oil.

Vidhi (procedure) :

Patient is advised to lie down in supine position and relax. Specially prepared ring is placed on the chest at cardiac region.

It is sealed properly with the help of dough prepared from black gram flour, so that no oil will leak out. Lukewarm oil is slowly poured in the socket. After approximately 25 minutes the oil is removed from the ring. Smooth massage is done with the remaining oil at the surface of cardiac region. The area is cleaned with gauze piece. Patient is advised to wear warm clothes and rest for a while.

Indications :

* Vatik hridroga, vatapaittik hridroga.

Hrid basti is associatary karma in Panchakarma therapy, It speeds up the results of curative ayurvedic medicinal treatment.

Kati Basti

Technique :

Kati basti is a special procedure included in group of allied karmas. This is not mentioned in Ayurveda samhitas but has been developed by vaidya - parampara i.e. innovation of basti.

Kati i.e. , lumbosacral region and surrounding part are the important sites of vata dosha.

Instruments Used :

Specially prepared ring, dough prepared from black gram flour, medicated oil and water.

Vidhi (Procedure) :

The specially prepared ring is properly sealed at, the portion of kati region, where there is pain . The ring is sealed with the dough of wheat and black gram flour. Lukewarm oil is poured in the ring so that swedan along with snehan is achieved. After approximately 25 minutes the oil is removed from the ring. Smooth massage is done with the remaing oil at the surface of kati region. The area is cleaned with gauze piece. Patient is advised to wear warm clothes and rest for a while.

Indications:

Sciatica

Osteoporosis

Intervertebral disc prolapse

Osteo arthritis

Restricted Muscular movements

Dhoomapana

Technique :

Dhoomapana is to inhale the medicated smoke. It is indicated mainly in diseases of kapha and vata dosha in head-neck region. It is also done as a post-operative procedure in vaman.

Instruments Used :

Dhoomanetra :

A pipe made of copper is used. Its dimensions are specifically mentioned. The broader end should be of the circumference of the thumb of that person. While other end should be of the circumference of the little finger.

Dhoomavarti (Wick) :

A wick of herbs (selection of herbs according to the doshas) is prepared in a specific way. For this purpose, a paste of herbs is prepared. It is applied on a stick/ blade of grass. When it dries, the stick on which the paste has been overlapped is removed.

Procedure :

1. Dhoomavarti is kept at the broader end of the dooomanetra and it is burnt. Smoke is inhaled from the other end.
2. Dhoomavarti is burnt and smoke is inhaled (in this procedure

dhoomanetra is not used). Smoke is inhaled by the nose through each nostril separately and is exhaled through mouth. If it is exhaled through nose - it leads to several diseases of eyes.

Types of Dhoomapana :

Name	Herbs Used	Dose	Kala (time)
Prayogic (Shaman)	Manjistha (Rubia cordifolia)	3 times in a day	After getting up in the morning
	Sariva (Haemidesmus indicus) Padmaka (Prunus cirasoidus)		After brushing After meals After sneezing
Snehan (mrudu)	Guggulu (Commiphera mukul) Jatamansi (Nordastachys) jatamansi) Usheer (Andropogom muricatus)	3 Apana (one apana is inhalation & exhalation) Till tears start coming from eyes.	Vata time (in the evening)
Shodhana (Teekshna-penetrating	Vidanga (Embelia ribes)	4 apana	After vaman, nasya
	Mareecha (Piper nigrum)		
	Pippali (Piper longum)		

<u>Signs and Symptoms of Proper Dhoomapana :</u>

- Feeling of clearance in the throat
- Symptoms of disease are relieved

Signs and Symptoms of Improper Dhoomapana (Ayoga) :

- Improper voice
- Stickiness in throat
- Heaviness in head

Signs and Symptoms of Excess Dhoomapana (Atiyoga) :

- Dryness, burning sensation in throat
- Bleeding through nose/mouth
- Thirst

Dhoomapana thus done regularly improves vision. One never suffers from cough, rhinitis, otalgia, headache. It gives fluency in speech.

Indications :

Heaviness in head

Headache

Migraine

Graying of hair, hairfall

Pain in eyes, otalgia

Locked jaw, stiffness in neck

Lack of taste, weak teeth

Hoarseness of voice

Sinusitis

Even if one uses medicines which are cooling in property, dhoompana should not be done in diseases of pitta dosha and rakta dhatu; since medicines are burnt and smoke is inhaled (it causes actual contact with heat, which aggrevates vitiation of pitta dosha and rakta dhatu).

Contraindications :

After administration of basti and virechan.

After intake of milk/curds/honey/alcohol.

Over exhausted person.

Angry, furious person.

Rakta pitta (bleeding through external orifices without external injury).

Anaemia

Vertigo

Unconsciousness

When the surrounding is too hot.

If dhoomapana is done in such cases, there may be aggrevation of disease. In that case pittaalleviating treatment is given.

Kawal and Gandush

Technique :

This is retaining medicated decoction/sneha/oil/ghee in the oral cavity.

In kawal, gargling is done.

In gandusha oral cavity is filled with decoction or sneha to its full extent and is held until desired symptoms are observed.

Procedure :

Fomentation should be done to neck and forehead. Material (decoction/oil/ghee) is held in the oral cavity looking slightly upwards till tears start coming and one feels secretion in the oral cavity.

Types : - Snehan, shaman, shodhan, and ropan

Name	Material used	Action
Snehan	Sneha (oil/ghee) Taste : Sweet, sour, (salty Lukewarm)	Mainly for vata dosha
Shamän	Cane-juice, milk, decoction of sweet root. (Cold)	Mainly for pitta dosha
Shodhän dosha	Decoctions Taste : Pungent Penetrating (Lukewarm)	Mainly for kapha (after nasya).
Ropan	Honey Cold	Mainly for mouth ulcers

Signs and Symptoms of Proper Kawal /Gandusha :

- Lightness in oral cavity
- Cleanliness in oral cavity

Signs and Symptoms of Improper Kawal /gandusha (Ayoga):

- Inability to identify the taste
- Vitiation of kapha dosha

Signs and Symptoms of Excess Kawal /gandusha (Atiyog):

- Stomatitis
- Thirst

These are mainly due to shodhana types of kawal/gandusha.

Seasame oil is used for kawal/gandusha when it is done daily.

Post operative :

- After kawal/gandusha patient is advised to drink hot water
- Light diet

Sleep is not advised immediately.

Indications :

- Diseases of oral cavity
- Stomatitis, weak teeth
- Dryness of mouth
- Excess salivation
- Lack of taste
- Otalgia
- Stiffness in neck

Gandusha is not to be done below the age of 6 years.

Shiro-abhyang (head massage)

Technique :

Head is the vital organ consisting of controlling centres of all the sense organs. It is the most important 'marma'. Head massage relieves all 'shirorogas' (it includes all types of headaches arising from different causes). Head massage relieves itching and dryness of scalp.

Moordh Taila :

i.e., application of oil to the head by various methods for a specific period.

Uses :

Prevents headache

Prevents falling and graying of hair

Gives sound sleep

Makes hair long and beautiful

There are four types/methods, which are progressively more and more effective i.e., Shiroabhyanga, shirodhara, shiropichu and shirobasti respectively.

Shirodhara

Technique :

Oil/ghee is poured in a drip over forehead for a specific time period

Instruments used :

Dharapatra (vessel) with a chain

A stand to which the chain is attached

A table

Oil/ghee/buttermilk

Cotton pads to cover the eyes

Procedure :

The room should be a calm and quiet place. For the disease of vata dosha oil/ghee should be lukewarm. For the disease of pitta the material should be of room temperature.

The patient is advised to lie down on the table. Two small cotton pads dipped in rose water are placed on the eyes. Oil/ghee is poured over forehead at a point just above the mid-point of eyebrows. It is done from the height of about four fingers. Drip should not be too slow or too fast.

Time period :

Half to one hour.

It is strictly to be done in the morning. After shirodhara medicated ghee is given orally according to the disease. Exertion is avoided.

Users :

- Increases memory, concentration
- Gives stability of mind
- Gives sound sleep
- Reduces body heat.

In similar fashion 'Takradhara' (dhara of butter milk) is also done.

Uses :

- Stops graying of hair
- Relieves exertion, headache
- Helps to cure the diseases of eye, ear.

Moordh Taila :

i.e. application of oil to the head by various methods for a specific period.

There are four types/methods, which are progressively more and more effective i.e. Shiroabhyanga, shirodhara, shiropichu and shirobasti respectively.

Shiro Pichu

Technique :

Gauze piece or a cloth is soaked in oil/ghee and is kept over the forehead/ant. Fontanelle.

Uses :

Stops falling/graying of hair.

Shirobasti

Technique :

It should be done only in the evening. Head should be shaved, cleaned to facilitate the procedure i.e., preventing leaking of oil. Special type of cap is prepared from leather which is put over the head and the lower end over the forehead is sealed by applying paste of black gram flour. Cap should be fixed properly. Oil is poured in it to accumulate upto the height of two fingers above the head. It is kept in the same position for the following duration.

Till the patient is relieved from the pain and secretion from nose and mouth start. Later oil is removed and massage is done to the head and shoulder region.

For disease of vata dosha - upto 10,000 matra = 51.6 minutes approximately

For disease of pitta dosha - upto 8,000 matra = 31.8 minutes approximately

For disease of kapha dosha - upto 6,000 matra = 26.9 minutes approximately

Indications :

Insomnia

Dryness in mouth, nose

Facial palsy

Migraine

Abhyanga

Abhi - surrounding

Anga - body

i.e., application of oil all over the body

It is advocated as a daily regimen. It alleviates vata dosha and fatigue, improves complexion.

Contraindications :

- Diseases of kapha dosha
- Indigestion
- Fever
- One who has undergone panchakarma therapy.

Time period :

When penetration of oil is expected upto rasa dhatu - abhyanga is done for 400 matra i.e., approximately 2.06 minutes.

500 matra - upto rakta dhatu, i.e. approximately 2.58 minutes.

600 matra for mansa dhatu, i.e. approximately 3.18 minutes.

700 matra for meda dhatu, i.e. approximately 3.61 minutes.

800 matra for asthi dhatu, i.e. approximately 4.13 minutes.

If not done to the whole body, Abhyang should at least be done to the head, ears and feet region daily. By abhyang to the feet region dryness is alleviated.

- Gives relief in physical exertion
- Improves vision
- Prevents cracking of feet
- One never suffers from sciatica

Udvartan

Rubbing of unctuous/dry medicated powders on the body is udvartan.

According to the property of powder it is of two types.

- Rooksha Udvartan (dry) - used in sthaulya (obesity). It alleviates kapha dosha and meda dhatu.
- Snigdha Udvartan (unctous) - This is used in Krusha (thin) patients and alleviates vata dosha.

Udvartan improves complexion, reduces body odour, relieves itching.

Mardan (Massage)

Technique :

Application of warm oil with heavy pressure is mardan. It is advised to be perform after Abhyanga and Udvartan. It is Useful in various diseases of vata dosha.

Procedure :

Various oils can be used according to the status of doshas :

Vata dominance : Narayan oil

Pitta dominance : Chandan bala lakshadi oil

Kapha dominance : Vishagarbha oil etc.

Action :

1. It alleviates muscular fatigue
2. It relieves muscle pain.
3. It creates feeling of lightness in the body.
4. It is recommended in various vata vyadhis.

Padaghat (feet massage)

Techniques :

Massage done by the feet is known as padaghat. This procedure generates more pressure as compared to mardan. Abhyang should necessarily be done prior to padaghat as it helps in better absorption of oil.

The therapist should not be over weight or very thin. His feet should be clean, soft and without any cracks.

Procedure :

Padaghat is performed by the technician, by taking support of two rings which are attached to the roof with the help of chains.

Action :

This procedure helps in strengthening the body. Vagbhat has advocated padaghat while explaining regimen in winter season. Sushrut has advocated padaghat as a daily regimen after Abhyang and exercise.

Parishek

Technique :

Pouring comfortably warm sneh i.e. (ghee/oil) over the body in a drip is parishek. It alleviates vata dosha. It relieves exertion. It helps in healing the wounds and fractures. Charak has advocated parishek of ghee in vatarakta (Gout).

Action :

1. It alleviates vata dosha.
2. Relieves exertion.
3. Helps in healing the wounds and fractures.

Indication :

1. Parishek of ghee in vatarakta (Gout)
2. Vatavyadhi
3. To relieve pain in wounds and burns.

Padabhyang

Abhyang is application of oil to the body. When abhyang is done only at the feet region it is termed as padabhyang. (pad-feet, abhyang - application of oil). The effects of padbhyang are as follows :

1. It alleviates the dryness, roughness, numbness and pain at the feet region.
2. It gives strength to the feet.
3. It helps to alleviate the cracks of the feet region and adds to the beauty of the feet.
4. It gives soothing effect to eyes and helps in improving the vision.
5. Regular padabhyang acts as a prevention against sciatica.
6. It gives proper tone to the muscles of the feet.

Dahan Karma (Agni-Karma)

Procedure :

This procedure is very helpful in some chronic & non curable diseases which generally the diseases which cannnot be cured by surgery or kshar karma, are relieved by dahan karma.

The exact location where dahan karma is to be done is marked. The shalaka is heated on the flame.

When it becomes red hot, it is touched at the desired location. It is kept in contact with the skin for ten seconds only.

After the procedure ghee is applied on the area of dahan karma.

Instruments :-

Agnikarma shalaka (a specially prepared instrument having the tip made from gold/copper/iron), ghee, Candle/lamp etc.

Indications :

Wart

Severe joint pain

Bleeding tendency

Contra indications:

Children

Sukumar

Pishichchil

Technique :

Powder of Amalaki *(Embelica officinale)*is mixed with water to form a pulp. This pulp is fixed at the anterior fontanelle with the help of gauze piece. This procedure is necessary for protection of head from excessive heat.

Patient is advised to lie down on the table. Four doctors perform this procedure at the same time. Each doctor has a piece of cloth in his hand. The cloth is dipped in warm oil and is then squeezed all over the body of the patient in a sinchronized manner. This oil is collected and reused after warming it.

According to doshas time period is as follows : -

Vata dosha - 2 hours

Pitta dosha - 1 hour

Kapha dosha - 1 hour

Pishichchil can be performed for 7/14/21/28 days depending on the status of doshas and general condition of patient.

Indications :

1. Vatavyadhi
2. External injury

3. Fracture
4. Pain

Pishichchil can be performed in healthy persons for maintenance of health. It strengthens the body, improves Agni(digestive power) and complexion. It gives stability to indriyas and prevents ageing.

Lepa

Indications :

Action of lepa differs as per the properties of its ingredients.

1. Inflammation
2. Pain
3. Facial palsy
4. Gout
5. Improving and maintaining the health of hair.
6. Improving complexion etc.

Technique : A paste is prepared by adding water to the herbal powder. Instead of water various other substances such as ghee, milk, honey, rose water etc. can be used. Patient is advised to sit on a chair by keeping the neck tilted backwards so that the face is in upward position. A towel is tied around the neck of the patient. Lepa is applied in upward direction. As lepa begins to dry, it should be removed with the help of a sponge soaked in water.

Pinda-sweda

Technique : This is a kind of fomentation with the help of cooked rice and milk. This is done after proper oleation to the body. These pottalies are dipped in the medicated milk which is hot in temperature (bearable to the body) and are rubbed all over the body in a circular motion. Body gets fomented. Paste of rice can be seen all over the body after this process. This treatment helps in alleviation of vata and gives proper tone to the muscles.

Indications :

1. Vatavyadhi
2. Immobility
3. Emaciation
4. Pain
5. Vata and Rakta Vitiation
6. Burning sensation etc.

10.
DISEASE AND PANCHAKARMA

10. Disease and Panchakarma

Hicca (Hiccup)

Etiological factors such as consumption of vidahi, heavy, abhishyandi, dry food etc. in excess, intake of cold food, cold drinks, suppression of natural urges, over exertion, atiyoga (excess) of vaman and virechan, pollution etc. cause vitiation of vata (pran and udan - types of vata) along with kapha. Vitiated vata afflicts liver, spleen, intestines, mouth and is then expelled out through mouth causing a typical deep pitched sound like hik-hik.

The usual treatment in Hicca in predominance of vata is snehan, swedan, virechan and nasya. In case of kapha predominance snehan, swedan and vaman along with dhoomapan is recommended.

Vata predominance	Snehan, swedan, virechan and nasya
Kapha predominance	Snehan, swedan, virechan, dhoomapan

Shwasa (Asthma):

Etiological factors such as intake of vidahi, heavy, abhishyandi and dry food in excess quantity, intake of cold food and drinks, suppression of natural urges, over exertion etc. cause vitiation of vata (pran and udan - types of vata) along with kapha. When the aggravated kapha, obstructs the normal path of vata, the vata moves in different directions in the body, then the process of breathing gets obstructed as a result of which shwasa (asthma) is manifested.

In strong patients when kapha is predominant, vaman is administered, following internal and external oleation and fomentation. Thus, the vitiated kapha is expelled out and the obstruction is cleared. Hence the normal direction of vata dosha is achieved.

Virechan is recommended in Tamakshwasa (a type of shwasa where vata is more predominant in the pathogenesis as compared to the types of shwasa). Expulsion of kapha and the normal direction of vata are achieved due to virechan as virechan has been recommended for alleviation of kapha and vata also.

Dhoom nasya is advised in case of residual kapha dosha after vaman.

Kapha dominance	Snehan, swedan, vaman
Vata dominance	Snehan, swedan, virechan

Amavata (Rheumatoid arthritis) :

Etioloical factors such as mutually contradictory food and regimens, lack of exercise etc. lead to formation of aam and vitiation of vata. This aam, being propelled by vata has affinity towards 'shleshma sthanas' (sites of kapha dosha). It further gets vitiated by vata, pitta and kapha and obstructs channels of circulation and causes heaviness in cardiac region and restricts body movements by causing stiffness all over the body.

Light diet along with deepan and paachan therapy is advised for the digestion of aam. Virechan is indicated after digestion of aam as it helps in elimination of vitiated vata dosha and also vitiated pitta and kapha dosha and gives proper direction (Anulom gati) to vata. Later, for pacification of the vitiated vata, snehapaan (intake of sneha) is advised followed by Anuvasn basti which contains saindhav (rock-salt)

Saamavastha (in the presence of Aam)	Paachan Chikitsa
Niraamavastha (after digestion of aam)	Virechan, internal snehan, anuvasan basti

Vata - Rakta (Gout) :

Generally in persons who have tender health, who indulge in wrong diet and regimen, who are obese and who lead a leisurely life, vata and rakta (blood) get vitiated due to factors like intake of very unctuous and hot food, indigestion, anger, sleeping during day time etc. Intake of vidahi food and riding an elephant, horse, camel etc. for a long duration cause vitiation of blood. Riding horse, elephant etc. for a long duration causes accumulation of blood in the legs as they remain in hanging position. This vitiated blood gets further vitiated by the aggravated vata as a result of which vata-rakta is manifested.

Vata-rakta is of two types : Uttana (superficial) and avagadha (deep-seated)

Uttana vata-rakta should be treated by lepa, abhyang and upanaha sweda. Virechana, Nirooha basti, and snehapana (intake of sneha) is advised for avagadha vata-rakta. Virechana helps in pacification of both, vitiated vata and rakta. Aasthapana basti and snehapana are advised for pacification of vitiated vata. Raktamokshana is advised for both types of vata-rakta.

Uttana	Lepa, abhyang, upanaha sweda
Avagadha	Internal snehan, virechan, Nirooha basti

Unmaada (Insanity and Demoniac seizures) :

Since the aggravated doshas cause impairment of the mental faculties, this psychic disorder is termed as unmaada. Shodhan (elimination) therapy is advised prior to any shaman (pacification) therapy. Snehapaan (intake of sneha) followed by virechan is adviced for vataja unmaada. Raktamokshan should be performed in pittaja unmaada, and vaman and virechan should be done in kapha - pittaja (dominance of kapha and pitta) unmaada. After the administration of above therapies

Nirooha, Anuvasan, Nasya, Abhyang, Dhoomapana and Snehappan are advised. Puraan Ghruta (very old ghee) is advised for nasya.

Kapha, pitta predominance	Vaman, virechan
Vata predominance	Internal snehan, virechan
Pitta predominance	Raktamokshan

Uru-stambha :

Etiological factors like intake of very heavy and over unctuous food, intake of mutually contradictory food, excessive exercise, excessive sleep etc. cause vitiation of kapha, vata, meda dhatu and formation of aam. When these morbid entities arrive in the thigh region, either or both thighs get afflicted and the bones of this region get filled up with vitiated kapha. As a result of this, thighs become immobile, cold and stiff. This condition is termed as urustambha. Treatment for alleviation of vata such as snehan, swedan may increase kapha and vice versa.

All the therapies of panchakarma are contra-indicated in this disease as vata and kapha, both are dominant in the pathogenesis and hence the treatment should be such that it should neither cause provocation of vata or kapha.

Visarpa (Erysepelas) :

Etiological factors like intake of saline, sour and pungent food cause aggravation of doshas and spread to different parts of the body to cause which is of seven types. Seven elements are involved in the manifestation of visarpa, viz, rakta, lasika (lymph), twak (skin), mansa (muscle tissues), vata, pitta and kapha.

Langhana (light diet/ fasting) and rookshana therapy is advised in the beginning which, corrects the vitiated rasa, and visarpa seldom occurs without the vitiation of rasa dhatu. Rakta and pitta are predominant factors in the pathogenesis of visarpa. Virechan and Raktamokshana are advised as they help in alleviation of both Vaman and lep are also recommended in this disease.

Visarpa	Virechan, vaman, lepa raktamokshan

Apasmara : (Epilepsy)

A condition characterised by black-outs, bewilderment, aggravation of doshas and loss of memory is called apasmara.

Vatika (vata-dominant) type of apasmara should be treated by basti, paittika type (pittadominant) of apasmara by virechan and kaphaja type (kapha-domianat) by vaman. The body of the patient should first be purified by elimination therapy and patient should be adequately consoled. Thereafter internal medications are advised. During the attack, pradhaman nasya is advised for regaining consciousness. Similarly strong anjan can be used for regaining consciousness.

Vata predominance	Basti
Pitta predominance	Virechan
Kapha predominance	Vaman

Ati sara :

Etiological factors such as indigestion of food, intake of viruddha (mutually contradictory) food ingredients, intake of food in excessive quantity, intake of dushta (polluted) water etc. causes vitiation of vata and adhatu (watery elements in the body). Vitiated vata causes downward movement of ab-dhatu which leads to suppression of agni (power of digestion) and liquidity of stools.

This stool mixed with ab-dhatu is expelled out throught the body due to stimulation of vata.

A patient of atisara should be treated according to the aam (presence of aam) and pakwa (after digestion of aam) stages of the disease. Stambhan chikitsa should not be administered in the aam-stage. If so done, the aam remains in the body and causes various complications. Hence in this stage, anuloman (mild laxatives) should be administered.

Deepan, paachan medicines are administered for paachan of aam. Later on stambhan medicines are advised in the pakwa stage. Anuvasan basti is advised in case of complications such as rectal prolapse, urine retention, pain in lumbar region etc.

In case of raktatisaar, i.e. stools with blood, pichha basti followed by anuvasan basti is advised.

Saamavasatha (Aam stage)	Anuloman, paachan
Niraamavastha (Pakwa stage)	Shaman Chikitsa
Raktatisaar	Pichha basti

Mootrashmari :

When vata afflicts urine along with shukra, pitta and kapha located in the basti (the term basti generally refers to urinary bladder, but in the present context it includes kidneys and ureters), ashmaris (stones) are formed gradually.

In the treatment snehan, swedan (avagaha), anuvasan basti and niruha basti can be used. In some cases even uttarbasti can be used.

As in the pathogenesis, vata is the vitiated dosha, the best treatment (as mentioned above) for vitiated vata is recommended.

Mootrashmari	Snehan, swedan, anuvasan basti, nirooha basti, uttar basti.

Rakta Pitta :

Etiological factors such as excessive indulgence in exercise, excessive grief, excessive walk etc. cause vitiation of pitta and pitta by its own attributes vitiates Rakta. As a result of this, bleeding takes place through upward tracts viz. nose, eyes, ears and mouth or downward tracts viz. urethra, vagina and anus or through both tracts including skin pores all over the body.

If the general condition of patient is good bleeding should not be stopped immediately as the vitiated rakta may cause various complications if not let out of the body. But the patient should be continuously under observation. Considering the general condition of the patient and status of rakta shodhan chikitsa should be administered.

The line of treatment of shodhan chikitsa should be such that it helps in ceasing the bleeding by changing the direction of the vitiated rakta. Hence, in urdhwaga (upward) raktapitta virechan is advised and vaman is advised to adhoga (downward) raktapitta. The shodhan chikitsa helps in elimination of vitiated doshas and vitiated rakta.

Urdhwaga	Virechan
Adhoga	Vaman

Kamala (jaundice) :

If a patient of pandu (anaemia) resorts to pitta-aggravating regimens in excess, his rakta (blood) and mansa dhatu get afflicted by vitiated-pitta. His eyes become excessively yellow and there may be yellowishness of skin, nails and face. The stool and urine of the patient become either red or yellow in colour or stool may be whitish in colour. His sense organs get afflicted and other symptoms like indigestion, weakness etc. are associated.

This condition caused by excessive aggravation of pitta is called kamala (jaundice). It is either located in koshta (alimentary tract) or shakha (tissue in the periphery) or both in koshtha and shakha.

The shodhan chikitsa varies in both the varieties of kamala. In bahupitta i.e. one located in koshtha, snehan (internal) followed by virechan is administered as vitiated pitta is the dominent factor of the pathogenesis and virechan is the best therapy for elimination of vitiated pitta.

In case of shakhashrita (located in the tissues of periphey) kamala snehan is not indicated as it may aggravate kapha dosha which is predominant in this type of kamala. Strong virechan is advised for elimination of vitiated kapha and pitta dosha.

Bahupitta	Internal snehan, virechan
Shakhashrita	Virechan

Kushtha :

The three vitiated doshas viz. vata, pitta and kapha in turn vitiate the twak (skin, in the present context plasma), rakta (blood), mansa (muscle tissue) and ambu (lymph). These taken together constitute the seven fold pathogenic substance of kushtha. In kushtha, if vata is predominant snehan (internal snehan), if kapha is predominant vaman and if pitta is predominant then rakta-mokshan and virechan therapies should be administered. To the patient suffering from kushtha, raktamokshana should be administered once in six months, virechan once every month, vaman therapy once in every fortnight and lepa should be applied once in three days.

Vata predominance	Internal snehan
Kapha predominance	Vaman
Pitta predominance	Raktamokshan, virechan

Udara Roga (Ascitis) :

Agni-mandya (decrease in digestive power) is the basic cause of every disease. But in case of udara roga agnimandya is specifically important cause. Due to agni-mandya aam is generated and this leads to obstruction of strotasas and accumulation of vitiated doshas and dhatus. They further obstruct mainly the strotasas of sweda, ambu (aqueous elements of the body) and vitiate prana and apan vayu (types of vata) as well as agni to produce udara roga.

As mentioned above, udara roga is caused by excessive accumulation of doshas and obstruction in strotasas. Hence virechan is advised daily. It not only helps in elimination of accumulated fluid, but also inhibits formation of new fluid.

Udara Roga	Virechan

Pandu (Aneamia) :

Etiological factors such as intake of excessive sour and saline food, excessive exercise, sleep during day time etc. cause vitiation of pitta. This vitiated pitta gets transmitted all over the body from the heart of various directions by vata. This vitiated pitta further vitiates kapha, vata, rakta, twak (skin) and mansadhatu. It causes pallor and/or discolouration to the skin. After ascertaining curability, the patient of pandu should be given snehan by administration of ghee. Thereafter, vaman and virechan therapies should be administered for elimination of vitiated doshas.

Kapha dominance	Snehan, Swedan, Vaman
Pitta dominance	Snehan, Swedan, Virechan

Pravahika :

Etiological factors such as indigestion of food, intake of viruddha (mutually contradictory) food ingredients, intake of food in excessive quantity, intake of dushta (polluted) water etc. agnimaandya and vitiation of vata and kapha doshas and formation of aam. The vitiated kapha is directed downwards towards pakvashaya by vitiated vata where it gets adhered to the internal walls of pakvashaya. Vata tries to expel this adhered kapha and hence the patient has to strain at the time of defecation. Very little kapha is expelled after much straining(pravahan).

Mrudu anuloman (mild laxatives) are advised in the aam stage (presence of aam) for removal of aam.

Later on pichha basti and anuvasan basti are administered. They help in alleviation of vata and swift expulsion of kapha dosha.

Saamavastha (presence of aam)	Anuloman, paachan chikitsa
Niraamavashtha	Pichha basti & Anuvasan basti

Prameha :

In this disease vitiation of kapha and meda is an important factor which gives symptoms like excess and turbid urination, burning sensation in hands and feet, excessive thirst, sweet taste in mouth etc. It is the vitiated kapha located in the basti (urinary bladder) which vitiates meda dhatu, mansa dhatu and kleda leading to prameha.

While treating prameha, prior to shaman chikitsa, sanshodhan (body purification) is done by vaman and virechan in healthy patients. By shodhan the vitiated kapha and pitta in the body get elimintated and this enhances the action of internal medicines (shaman chikitsa).

Prameha	Vaman, virechan

Pratishyaya :

Indigestion, suppression of natural urges, exposure to dust, sleeping in daytime, excessive use of cold water, excessive indulgence in sex, consumption of abhishyandi food may cause pratishyaya.

Vitiated vata gets accumulated in the head region (which is one of the sites of kapha dosha) either individually or in association with other doshas including rakta dhatu causing pratishyaya. The signs and symptoms observed are sneezing, heaviness in head, etc.

Pradhaman nasya is used to alleviate vitiated doshas and to clear the srotas. Vaman is also indicated for elimination of vitiated dosha in chronic condition.

Pratishyaya	Pradhaman nasya, vaman

Kasa (cough) :

Etiological factors such as consumption of vidahi, heavy abhishyandi, dry food etc. in excess. Excessive intake of cold food, cold drinks, suppression of natural urges, over exertion etc. cause vitiation of vata and kapha. In the pathogenesis vitiated vata, especially apan vata (a type of vata) loses its normal downward direction and gets activated in upward direction. Udan vayu (a type of vata dosha having its normal direction - upwards) enhances the force of apan vayu. This upward force disturbs the normal direction (downwards) of prana vayu causing kasa.

Snehan and swedan play a major role in the treatment of kasa. In kapha predominant kasa vaman can be administered. Virechan also helps in normalizing the direction of vitiated vata dosha.

Kapha predominance	Snehan, swedan, vaman
Vata predominance	Snehan, swedan, virechan

Vatavyadhi :

Strotasas get vitiated by aggravated vata causing vata vyadhi.

Vatavyadhi comprises of pakshaghata (palsy), ardita (bells palsy), Sandhigatavata (Osteoarthritis) etc.

Pakshahghata : It is the Pranavayu, which when vitiated affects the halt part of the body by depleting unctuousness of that side of the body.

As here Pranava loses its normal direction, snehan, swedan and virechan are recommended to bring pranavayu to normal. Similar time of treatment is recommended in case of ardita as the pathogenesis is similar.

In Sandhigata vata the vitiated vata dosha afflicts the joints by depleting the unctuousness necessary at the site. The causes pain, oedema at the joints. In treatment snehan & swedan play a major role along with virechan.

Vatavyadhi : Snehan, Swedan, Virechan.

Arsha (Haemorrhoids)

Agni maandya (Suppression of digestive power) or other etiological factors such as suppression of natural urges like micturation or defection leads to vitiation of doshas. The vitiated doshas cause vitiation of twak (skin), mansa dhatu & meda dhatu which further causes occurence of Mansankuras (growths) at the anal region i.e. : Arsha.

Anuvasan basti is indicated when vata is predominant in the samprapti (pathogenesis). Nirooha basti is indicated when sticky secretions occur from the Arsha as a major symptom.

Snehan & Swedan (oleation & fomentation) should be done when pain and oedema is associated with Arsha.

Virechan is advised wihen Pitta & Kapha doshas are predominant in the pathogenesis. In case of bleeding through Arsha, it should not be stopped immediately. On the other hand (blood-letting) Raktamokshan therapy should be performed for the elimination of remaining vitiated blood. If the vitiated blood is retained in the body, it may cause colic pain, anaha (constipation associated with distension of abdomen) & more bleeding. Pichha basti is indicated to stop the bleeding if the bleeding does not stop by other means (when the blood is pure & not vitiated).

Vata predominance	Sheahan, swedan, Anuvasan & Nirooha basi
Kapha/pitta predominance	Virechan
Bleeding piles	Raktamokshan, Pichha basti

Chhardi (Vomiting)

Etiological factors such as intake of more amount of liquids or intake of food which is unaccustomed to the body etc. lead to vitiation of vyan & udan vayu (Types of vata) & further stimulate Kapha & pitta dosha which causes nausea & further chhardi (vomiting). Indigestion is an important factor in the pathogenesis of chhardi. Also the normal direction of doshas is lost. So, for elimination of vitiated doshas & to give proper direction to doshas in the body, Virechan is administered.

But, if the doshas are accumulated in the stomach or if kapha dosha is dominant in the pathogenesis, then mild vaman is indicated for elimination of doshas, as mouth is the nearest route for elimination of doshas which are accumulated in the stomach.

Pitta, vata dominance	Virechan
Kapha dominance	Mild vaman

Shotha (Oedema)

Etiological factors such as intake of mutually contradictory ingredients of good and polluted as well as poisonous food, affliction by piles, difficulty in labour, etc. lead to vitiation of vata.

The aggravated vata afflicts rakta (blood), pitta & kapha and carry these vitiated elements to vessels in the exterior part of the body. In the twak (skin) & mansa dhatu, vata itself gets obstructed by these vitiated elements as a result of which shotha (oedema) is manifested.

Langhan & Pachan should be done in case of 'Aam induced shotha'. Virechan should be done after Langhan & Pachan for the removal of vitiated doshas.

Nasya should be done when shotha is manifested in the head region.

When shotha is manifested in the lower region of the body, virechan should be performed.

Vaman is advised when shotha is manifested in the upper region of the body.

The above panchakarma therapies have been advised for elimination of vitiated doshas via nearest route i.e. nose, mouth or anus.

Samavastha	Pachan
Niramavastha	Virechan Sotha in lower region -> Virechan Sotha in upper region -> Vaman Sotha in head -> Nasya

Amla - Pitta

Intake of food which causes vitiation of pitta dosha causes accumulation of vitiated pitta dosha in the body. Further continuation of etiological factors leads to Amla-pitta causing various symptoms like indigestion, heart burn, head-ache etc.

As the important factor in the pathogenesis is accumulation of pitta dosha in amashay (stomach) the elimination of doshas is very important in the line of treatment. Hence Vaman should be administered as it is the nearest route for elimination of pitta dosha via amashay (stomach). Virechan should also be performed for the elimination of residual doshas if necessary.

Amlapitta	Vaman, Virechan

❖❖❖

11

PREPARATION OF OILS AND MEDICINES

11. Preparation of Oils and Medicines

Ingredients :

In panchakarma, various oils and medicines are used which differ according to the doshas/diseases. But the basic method of preparation is the same. The basic ingredients and the instruments are as follows :

Oils/Ghees

To prepare any medicated oil or ghee the base may be sesame oil, coconut oil or mustard oil. Sesame oil is widely used, due to its multi fold properties. Ghee prepared from cow's or buffalo's milk can be used. Usually cow's milk is preferred.

Medicines proposed : The medicines to be used for the preparation of oil can be taken in the form of decoction, dry form or juice etc.

For cooking purpose, stove or heater can be used.

A piece of cloth or a proper filter can be used for the purpose of filteration.

Technique :

For the preparation of oil, ingredients to be used should be in the proportion of 1:4:16 i.e.

Medicine - 1 part

Oil/Ghee - 4 parts

Water - 16 parts

Method of Preparation :

Oil / ghee can be prepared by two methods which are as follows:

In this method, medicine, oil/ghee and water are mixed together in the proportion 1:4:16 respectively. Heat is given to the mixture, till the water inside gets evaporated completely. Then the oil/ghee is Filtered to get the final product. Usually the first method is used when the medicine is in the powdered form.

Criteria for properly prepared oil/ghee :

The procedure should be ended after observing the following symptoms :

1. Oil preparation - froth starts appearing; Ghee preparation - when the froth gets completely disapeared.

2. A piece of paper dipped into the prepared oil/ghee when burnt, burns without sparkling.

3. Odour and colour of the medicines reflect in the oil.

4. Properly prepared oil/ghee when applied on the skin forms a thin unctuous layer on the skin.

Application :

A. Routes of administration :

1. Oral
2. Nasal
3. Anal
4. Per-vaginal in female
   Per-urethral in male
5. Gandush
6. Kaval
7. Abhyang
8. Shiro-abhyang
9. Shiro-pichu
10. Shiro-dhara

11. Shiro-basti
12. Netra-basti
13. Karna-pooran

B Treatment :

1. Shodhan
2. Shaman

The properties of oil being opposite to the properties of vata dosha help in alleviating vata.

Different kinds of oils can be used in various disorders of vitiated vata. e.g. sandhigata vata (osteo arthritis), shwasa (asthama), kasa (cough), muscular dystrophy etc.

Oils/ghee medicated with herbs that alleviate kapha or pitta can be used in various kapha or pitta disorders.

12
ANCIENT METHODS AND MODIFICATIONS

12. Ancient Methods and Modifications

Ayurveda is an ancient science. The instruments/apparatus that have been described in the Ayurvedic texts are according to the life-style or technique that was in use at that time period. But, as the years have passed, the development has been made by man in various fields which is todays necessity.

In this aspect, modification of the various instruments used for panchakarma therapy is also very necessary for the sake of convenience and time consumption. But while the modification is being made, the basic principles of Ayurveda should remain unchanged.

Basti :

Ancient : The ancient method of administration of basti is with the urinary bladder (Basti putak) of an animal. The urinary bladder should be of a bull or buffalo. This bladder should be tanned and should be free from foul smell. It should not be very unctuous, very thick or very thin. Administration of basti using the instrument is by squeezing the basti putak. This should be done in a proper manner.

Basti netra should not be too long, too short or sharp. Basti netra should be properly tied to the basti-putak. All these rules should be followed thoroughly otherwise it may create various complications. Moreover, this method is very inconvenient and time consuming.

Modification : Instead of this instrument, enema pot with a rubber tube and catheter can be used. The merits of this modification are that we can use in the sterilized form; it can be conveniently made available all over the world. This method has simplicity and is time saving as compared in the ancient method. Similarly for anuvasan basti we can use syringe and catheter in sterlized form.

Shirodhara :

Ancient : Earthen pot is being used traditionally for the purpose of shirodhara. Copper or iron pots can be used as a substitute for the earthen pot.

Modification : A modified instrument for the purpose of shirodhara is being used nowadays. It consists of a tube through which dhara is held on the fore head. This tube is attached to a vessel containing the liquid used for shirodhara. Merits of this method are that the liquid is circulated automatically by a pump attached to the vessel. Heating system installed in this instrument regulates temperature of the liquid.

Raktamokshan :

Ancient : siravyadha - the aim in this method is to ooze out the blood from a vein. Traditionally it is done with a sharp instrument by giving a small cut to a vein.

Modification : With the help of needle and syringe the blood can be taken out with a vein. By using the needle and syringe we can minimize the pain and take out the desired amount of blood from the vein.

Nasya :

Ancient : For nasya, cotton swab soaked in medicine is squeezed in each naostril.

Modification : Instead of this method one can use the dropper made from glass or plastic. With the help of a dropper it becomes easy and more convenient.

Nadi-Sweda :

Ancient : It is a type of swedan where foementation can be done to a localized part of the body. An earthen pot containing medicinal decoction and a tube attached to it is used for nadi-sweda. Steam formed in the vessel passes through the tube and foementation is done with this steam.

Modification : A pressure-cooker with a rubber tube attached to its lid is used for the purpose. The medicinal decoction can be prepared in it by attaching an electrical cord to it.

Pradhaman Nasya :

Ancient : Previously a cone made from paper was used for the purpose of pradhman nasya. Drawback of this method is that skill of the doctor plays an important role. Slight mistake in administration of nasya may create complications.

Modification : Modified instrument consists of a ruber tube with a ballon attached to it. A plastic vessel containing the medicinal powder is attached to the distal end of the tube. The powder is blown in the nostrill by pumping the ballon. Administration of nasya is made easier and more convenient with the help of this instrument.

Khalbatta (Pestie - Mortar) :

Ancient method : Drawback of this instrument is that it should be used manually and hence it is a time consuming process.

Modification : In the modified instrument motor is attached to the pestle. Here man power and time is saved.

Swedan Peti (Steam - box) :

Ancient : the ancient procedure is very tedious and time consuming. Patient is advised to lie on a cot which is placed above a pit. Swedan is performed by fumes produced from the medicines burnt in the pit.

Modification : Modified instrument consists of a wooden box which has two compartments at its base. Two vessels with electrical coils are kept in these compartments. Patient is advised to lie in the upper compartment. Swedan is performed by steam produced from the medicinial decoction contained in the vessels. Position of patient is such that his head remains out of the box on a platform. The box is designed in such a manner that when it is closed, steam can not escape from any place. This is a very convenient method in which the time period of swedan can be regulated easily.

This is a multipurpose box in which the upper most platform can be used for the purpose of snehan. Shirodhara can also be performed in this box.

Netrabasti :

Ancient : To remain sneh at the eye, dough made from black gram flours is encircled around the eye so as to prevent any leakage of sneha.

Sneha may leak out from the socket if the dough is not of proper consistency. This is a skillfull job. Similar procedure is performed for katibasti & Hridbasti.

Modification : A specially prepared eye cap is used to form a socket in which the sneha is retained. It is sealed externally so as to prevent any leakage. The chances of error are minimised due to this modification. Similarly specially prepared metal ring serves the purpose as a modification in Katibasti and Hridbasti.

13.

QUESTIONS & ANSWERS

13. Questions & Answers

Karma

How does Nasya work ?

All the indriyas (i.e. the controlling centres of the sense organs) are situated in the head. They are concentrated at a particular point i.e. Shrungatak marma. The Nasal route is the nearest route to this marma. Hence, the medicine administered by nasya acts on all indriyas via Shrungatak marma.

Can snehan and swedan be included in Panchakarma ?

Snehan and swedan lead to separation of doshas from their substratum and divert them towards koshtha from where they are expelled out by elimination therapies of panchakarma. Hence they can be included in the poorvakarma, but not as the main procedures of panchakarma.

What are karma, kala and yoga basti ?

According to the number of basties to be given, they are of three types, viz. karma basti, kala basti, and yoga basti. In karma bati 30 basties are given : on the first day, 1 anuvasan, 12 nirooha and 12 anuvasan alternately and in the end 5 anuvasan. In the kala basti a total of 16 basties are given. On the first day, 1 anuvasan, 6 nirooha & 6 anuvasan alternately and in the end 3 anuvasan. In yoga basti 8 basties are given. First basti is anuvasan, then 3 nirooha and 3 anuvasan alternately and in the end 1 anuvasan. These basties are recommended according to the desired period of the treatment.

What are the rules to be followed during snehan ?

Sneha should be taken on an empty stomach at around 7 AM. The patient should have food only when he is truly hungry. Lukewarm water should be used for all purposes. Natural urges should not be suppressed. Over exertion, daytime sleep & night vigil should be avoided. A Fresh, warm and light meal is advised.

Can virechan be divided into catagories ?

Virechan has been divided into four categories according to the mode of action by Sharangdhar. Anuloman : These are the medicines which cause digestion of the malas and bring them downwards by breaking the adherence eg. Haritaki (Terminalia chebula). Sransan : The digested indigested malas which are adhered to the internal walls of the alimentary canal are brought in the downward tract e.g. Aragwadha (Cassia fistola)

Bhedan : This is the process where the formed/semi solid/watery stools are disintegrated and brought downwards eg. Katuka (Picrorrhiza kurroa) Rechan : The medicines which cause elimination of digested/indigested malas by bringing them to liquid form are termed as rechan eg. Trivrut (Operculina terpetham).

Explain the action of vaman dravyas'.

Ushna & teeksha properties -> Disintegration and liquification of doshas. Sookshma -> Penetration through srotasas and diversion of doshas towards aamashay. Dominance of tej and vayu mahabhut -> Doshas are directed upward due to the normal tendency of these mahabhutas and by stimulation of udan vayu.

Explain the action of virechan dravyas ?

Ushna & teekshna -> Disintegration and liquification of doshas. Sookshma -> Penetration through srotasas and diversion towards pakwashay. Dominance of prithvi & aap mahabhut in the medicines -> Doshas are directed downwards due to the normal tendency of these mahabhutas and by stimulation of apan vayu.

Explain sneha pan vidhi.

For sneha pan the oil/ghee is chosen according to the disease. Just after sunrise the sneha should be taken on an empty stomach. On the first day sneha should be 25 gm and then it should be increased gradually. In case of digestive power is strong, the dose of sneha should start from 50 gm and should be increased gradually upto 300 gm on the seventh day. If symptoms like nausea and vomiting, persist at the time of snehapan, then warm water or yusha can be used as anupan. Symptoms of optimum snehan are : loose stools, unctuousness all over the body, unctuous stools etc.

Explain the action of basti.

Properly administered basti is retained at the site of pakwashay, pelvic area and under the level of the umbilicus. The respective actions of basti dravyas such as shodhan, shaman etc. are observed all over the body due to their veerya.

Diet

What is maansarasa ?

Mansarasa is a preparation like soup where meat pieces are cooked with water. The proportion of water and meat pieces can be of these types : 320 gm. meat & 640 gm. water, 240 gm. meat & 640 gm. water, or 160 gm. meat & 640 gm. water. The water should be reduced to 1/4th & meat should cook. These preparations are progressively easier to digest.

What is Yavagu ?

Manda, peya & vilepi together constitute Yavagu. The Proportion of raw rice or other cereals like (wheat etc.) is the same in all three preparations i.e. it should be 1/4th of the quantity needed in the normal diet. The Proportion of water increases in vilepi, peya & manda and hence they are easier to digest respectively.

What is Manda ?

The Proportion of medicated water should be fourteen times that of the rice. When the rice is cooked, only the liquid portion is used for the diet and this is termed manda.

What is peya ?

The proportion of medicated water is six times that of the rice. After the rice is cooked more partion of liquid along with a very small partion of cooked rice is used for dietary purposes. This is termed peya.

What is vilepi ?

The Proportion of medicated water is four times that of the rice. After the rice is cooked, larger proportion of rice and comparatively less water is used for dietary purposes. This is vilepi.

What is mantha ?

Mantha is the preparation used for tarpana. It is prepared in the following way : 40 gm. of barley is mixed with about one tablespoon of ghee. 160 gm. of water is added to this and the mixture is blended thoroughly. Sugar, honey and jaggery are added to it and this mixture is called mantha.

What is yusha ?

The Recipe of yusha is similar to soup where medicinal herbs, pulses & liquid such as water, buttermilk, medicinal decoction etc. are cooked together. The proportion of these ingredients is as follows : 10/20 or 40 gms of medicinal herbs, 40 to 80 gms of pulses and 640 gm of liquid. This liquid reduced to 1/4th part is yusha.

What is kruta & akruta yusha ?

Yusha processed with digestive stimulants such as Piper nigum etc. is termed kruta yusha. Plain yusha without any digestive stimulants is called akruta yusha.

Diseases

Action of panchakarma in various diseases.

Doshas & dushyas commingle in various patterns & manifest various diseases. Principle of treatment is the separation of these two factors and bringing them to normal status. Elimination therapies in panchakarma help in the expulsion of vitiated doshas & subsequently give normalcy to the dushyas.

Why virechan is recommended in Tamak shwas ?

Though vitiation of kapha & vata is a common factor in pathogenesis of shwasa, vata is predominant in Tamak shwas. Hence instead of vaman, virechan is recommended. It helps in the expulsion of kapha from Amashaya which is the basic site in the pathogenesis of Tamak shwas & it also give normal direction to vata.

Please explain the action of Virechan in Pakshaghat.

Action of virechan in Pakshaaghata (paralysis).

Vitiated vata and rakta manifest as Pakshaaghaata. Rakta & a major part of pitta exist in a commingled state. Hence virechan the recommended treatment for pitta is also effective of vitiated rakta. Virechan in pakshaaghata gives normalcy to pitta & subsequently rakta. The normal direction of vata is also achieved.

How shirodhara can be beneficial in the management of stress?

The Affliction of indriyas by vitiated vata is the basic factor in the manifestation of stress.

Shirodhara, a type of snehan is directed on the head region which is the basic site of all indriyas. Normalcy of vata is achieved as snehan is the best treatment for vata. Snehan also gives nourishment to the indriyas.

14.
DOCTOR'S LIST

14. Doctors' List

1) Dr. P.H. Kulkarni
Ayurveda Academy / Institute of Indian Medicine
36, Kothrud, Opp. Mhatoba Temple,
Pune - 411 029. M.S. India
Tel. : (091)(020) 332130, 343933
Telefax : (091) (020) 343933
Email : sagar.kulkarni@gems.vsnl.net.in

2) Dr.(Mrs.) P.M. Akkalkotkar
'Shubhankar"
680, Sadashiv Peth, Kumthekar Road,
Near Sadashiv Peth Post Office,
Pune - 411 030. M.S. India
Tel. : (091)(020) 4492663

3. Dr. K.V. Shah
Rashtriya Shikshan Mandal
Ayurved Rasashala Campus,
25, Karve Road,
Pune - 411 004. M.S. India

4. Dr. S.N. Parachure
Rashtriya Shikshan Mandal
Ayurved Rasashala Campus,
25, Karve Road,
Pune - 411 004. M.S. India

5. Dr. V.V. Doiphode
Chintamani Apartments,
1025 B, Sadashiv Peth,
Pune - 411 030. M.S. India
Tel : 4470225

6. Dr. B.B. Date
   Nanal Hospital
   Ayurved Rasashala Campus,
   25, Karve Road,
   Pune - 411 004. M.S. India.

7. Dr.Sadanand Deshpande
   Kayachikitsa Department,
   Tilak Ayurved College,
   Rasta Peth, Near Daruwala Bridge,
   Pune - 411 011. M.S. India

8. Dr.Mandar Akkalkotkar
   Ayurved Rasashala Campus,
   25, Karve Road,
   Pune - 411 004. M.S. India
   Tel. : (091)(020) 366087

9. Vd.Yogesh Bendale
   A/4, Ramyanagari Housing Society,
   Near Suhag Mangal Karyalaya,
   Bibwewadi, Pune, M.S. India
   Tel. : (091) (020) 4216273 / 365886
   Fax : (091) (020) 361942

10. Vd.(Mrs.) Vineeta Bendale
    Flat No. 1 & 2, Shree Vijay Apts.,
    Neelkamal Society, Karve Nagar,
    Pune - 411 052. M.S. India
    Tel : (091) (020) 365886
    Fax : (091) (020) 361942

11. Vd. Ghanashyam Marda
Ayurved Research Instt.
25, Karve Road,
Pune - 411 004. M.S. India
Tel : (091) (020) 341744 / 353021
Email : ghanashyam_marda@yahoo.com

12. Vd. Neeta Hinge
'Yashodeep', 44/6, Navasahyadri Society,
Karve Nagar, Opp. Post Office,
Pune - 411 052. M.S. India
Tel : (091) (020) 341070

13. Vd. (Mrs.) Prachiti Patwardhan
B-3, Prajakta Apts.,
Near Vitthal Mandir, Karve Nagar,
Pune - 411 052. M.S. India

14. Vd. Mahesh Sabade
'Kalaniwas'
1950, Sadashiv Peth, Madiwale Colony,
Pune - 411 030. M.S. India
Tel : (091)(020) 4477394
Fax : (091) (020) 4476451
Email : mahesh_sabade@usa.net

15. Vd. (Mrs.) Madhura Bhide
53, Mayur Colony,
3, Shriniwas Apts., Kothrud,
Pune - 411 029. M.S. India
Tel : (091)(020) 343508

16. Vd. Yogesh Kale
    102/3, Shramik Nagar,
    7/1, 'Narmada'
    Behind Shiwaji Housing Society,
    Pune - 411 016. M.S. India
    Tel : (091)(020) 5655910
    E-mail - yogesh_kale@yahoo.com

17. Vd. (Mrs.) Manjiri Kulkarni
    A-21/16, Swaroop Society,
    Near Mehandale Garage,
    Erandavane, Pune. M.S. India
    Tel : (091) (020) 360101

18. Dr. P.K. Dharmapalan
    Reader
    Dept. of Kayachikitsa
    Vaidyaratnam Ayurveda College
    Oiiyr Thaikkatt Ussery
    Thrissur
    Kerala

19. P. Ramchandra Nair
    Visinu Pharmaceuticals
    Nursing Home
    Pattambi Road
    P.O. Govt. Press
    Sharannur
    Kerala

20. Vd. Shailesh Nadkarni
    4/18, Navjivan Society,
    Lamington Road,
    Mumbai - 400 008.

21. Dr.B.R. Lalitha
    No.4, Chickanna Cottages
    Loopiane of Race Course Road
    Bangalore 560 009

22. Dr.Bhaskar V. Sathye
    Principal
    Gomantak Ayurveda Mahavidyalaya
    Shiroda
    Goa 403 103.

23. Dr.P.S. Pawar
    Gangadhar Shastri Gune
    Ayurveda Mahavidyalaya
    A'Nagar.

24. Prof. Dr. A.R. Shitre
    Mahvoner Corner,
    Savedi Road,
    Gune Ayurvedic Mahavidyalaya
    A'Nagar.

25. Dr. Dhananjay Khasgiwale,
    570, Narayan Peth,
    Near Kesari Office,
    Pune - 411 030.
    Ph. No. - 4452885

15.
PANCHAKARMA WORLDWIDE

15. Panchakarma Worldwide

1. Farida Irani
   80, Coonara Avenue
   West Penn Ant. Hills
   NSW 2125
   Australia

2. Dr.Krishna Kumar
   Austral Erba
   Herbal Products and Spagyric Laboratories
   2T, Blight Street Ridifyton
   S. Australia 5008

3. David Timbs
   113, Gladston Road
   Gibborn, New Zealand

4. Dr. Dinesh Varsani
   8, Batu Batu Garden
   1st Park Lands
   P.O. Box 34715
   Nairobi, Kenya (East Africa)

5. Swami Joythimayananda
   Presidente C. Cyctural
   16126 Geniva
   Via BALBI 33/29 Italy

6. Dr. Massimo Moresi
   Via. ROME - 647500/05
   Donato - in - Cullina
   Florence, Italy

7. H.H. Swami Yoga Anand Bharati
Apma International
24 Ave Jean Moulin
75014 Paris
France

8. Dr. Scott Gerson
Ayurvedic Medicineo of New York
Suite - 1
13 West 9th Street
New York, NY 10011
USA

9. Dr. Rani Pargaonkar
Herbal Nutrint Supplent
Ayurvedic Medicine
7895 Boaway
Merrillville
I.N. 46410
USA

10. Dr. Mauroof M. Athique
20, Annes Grove
Great Linford
Milton Keynes, MK 145 DR
England

11. Dr. E.B.S. Premdani
Rijksstraatweg 195
3956 CM LEERSUM
Netherlands

16.

BOOKS

16. Books

1. Divakar Ojha & Ashok Kumar, Panchakarma Therapy in Ayurveda.

General concept of Panchakarma therapy has been described in this book. One can come across historical aspect like references of Panchakarma in Vedas, Brahaman Granthas, Greek medicine etc. Snehan, swedan and the five therapies of Panchakarma have been elaborately described. Glossary of scientific terms has been given for reader's assistance.

2. T.L. Devraj, The Panchakarma Treatment of Ayurveda

Alongwith the snehan, swedan, the Panchakarma therapies have described in detail. Photos are inserted to make the book more beneficial and authentic on the utility of Panchamkarma in practice. Some modified types of swedan like Panchakizi etc. which are practised in south-India have also been explained in this book.

3. R.H. Singh, Panchakarma Therapy

This book gives elaborate description about the five therapies of Panchakarma. Snehan and swedan have been described in details. Allied karmas such as shirodhara, shirobastj etc. have been described along with few modifications.

4. Books in Marathi language :

a. Vd. Athavale, Ayurvediya Panchakarma Vidnyan
b. D.S. Kelkar, Ayurvedatil Panchakarma (Panchakarma in Ayurveda)
c. Dr. Subhash Ranade, Ayurvediya Panchakarma (with Rasayana Vajikarana)
d. Dr. Prabnhu, Panchakarmachi Olakha (Introduction to Panchakarma)

e. Vd. Y.G. Joshi, Ayurvediya Panchakarma Vidnyan

5. In Hindi language
a. Vd. Santosh Mishra, Sugama Panchakarma evam Prakrutic Chikitsa (Panchakarma & Naturopathy)
b. Dr. T.L. Devraj, Keraliya Panchakarma Chikitsa Vidnyan
c. Acharya Mukundilal Dvivedi (Edited), Ayurvediya Panchakarma Chikitsa
d. Vd. Kasture, Ayurvediya Panchakarma Vidnyan.

17.
THESIS

17. Thesis

Role of local Snehan in garbhini paricharya (natural care)

Local Snehan helps in gaining proper tone at the vaginal & cervical region. This includes normal labour without any complications.

Only primi and second para patients who have completed 32 weeks of pregnancy were selected.

Pichu of sesame oil was administered in the vaginal path every three days. This was continued until introduction of labour.

The cervix was dilated with the help of sesame oil in the second statge of labour Approximately 40 cc oil was needed for each patient.

The treatment helps in dilatation of cervix by gaining proper tone.

The labour is made easier due to proper dilation of vaginal path. This minimizes the chances of tear and episiotomy. Episioto my was prevented even in primi para.

To study the efficiency of uttar - basti of Nimba Patra (Aradirachta) decoction on kaphaja yoni vyapdda.

Symptoms like Leucorrhea, itching of vaginal region etc. are seen in kaphaja yoni vyapada. Uttar basti of Nimba patra decoction was administered for seven days. Necessary examination & investigations were done.

Complete relief was observed gradually in Leucorrhea & vaginal itching within seven days.

Kaphaj pratishyaya & its treatment especially Nasya Chiki'sa

Pratishyaya is very common & troublesome disease.

In this project vacha tail was selected for virechana nasya as a treatment for pratishyaya.

Vacha helps in alleviation of vata & kapha, is not potent & is urdhwabhagahara.

Duration of treatment was 7 days, 3 times a day - 3 drops in each nostrial.

Vacha tail nasya chikitsa on Kapha pratishaya shows good results, gives fast relief & is most useful treatment without side effects.

Study on Balapakshayhata (Poliomyelitis) & its management by Panchakarma Therapy.

The aim was to assess improvement in the strength of muscles in term of muscle power & to find proptylactic measures in preventing the incidence of poliomyelitis.

Material used :

Matra Basti : Mahabala Tail 30 ml.

Pinda Sweda : Balamoola powder - 250 gm.

Water : 4 litre

Rice : 1 kg.

Milk : 4 litre

2 pieces of cloth

Observations & conclusion :

1. Prevalence is more in male children (63.7%)
2. 5% increase in body weight in all cases in the course of treatment was noticed.
3. Hip extensor of left side affected cases were improved.

4. No complications or side effects of basti treatment were noted.
5. All cases agined muscle power in each treatment.

The management of vishvachi with special reference to Nasya chikitsa.

Main symptoms of vishwachi are restricted movements & pain at arm region Drug selection : Mashadi tail was used for nasya as pratimarsha nasya.

Total duration : 14 days.

Observation :

1.	Functional assessment	67.9 % Relief	
2.	Total cure	17 Patients	42%
	Marked improvement	12 Patients	30%
	Improved	9 Patients	22.5%
	Stable condition	2 Patients	5%

Conclusion : Vishwachi can be effective managed with the use of nasya of Mashadi tail.

The effect of ghruta nasya in the management of ardhawabhedak.

Ardhavabhedak is a disease similer to migraine. Modern medicine has its own limitations for the treatment as this disease. This is an attempt to find out a useful Ayurvedic remedy for ardhavabhedak.

Drug used - Goghruta (cow's ghee) Nasya

2 drops three times a day (7 am - 2 am - 9 pm)

Total Duration - 3 months

Conclusion :

Simple treatment of goghruta nasya gives relief to a considerable extent.

To study the efficacy of swedan in vatavyadhi.

Swedam is one of the most effective treatments for alleviation of vitiated vata.

Diseases such as Pakshaghata (paralysis), Aardita (Facial palsy), Grudhrasi (sciatica), jeerna sandhigata vata (chronic osteo arthritis) etc. were included in this study.

Snigdha (unctuoas) / Ruksha (dry) sweda was given according to the stage of the disease.

Conclusion :

Relief was observed in symptoms like heaviness, stiffness, tremors etc.

Out of total 50 patients pain was a common symptom in 44 patients.

40 Patients were relieved while four patients did not get the relief with the treatment.

Four patients showed symptoms of excessive swelling like weakness giddiness etc.

To study the efficacy of snehan swedan in Shwas & Hikka.

Shwas & Hikka originate at the site of kapha and vata plays a important role in the pathogenesis of these diseases.

Hence this project is undertaken to study the efficacy of snehan swedan on kapha & vata and hence shwas & hikka.

Drugs used snehan - seasame oil.

Narayan tail for weak patients.

Swedan - hair dryer, hotwater bag, Nadiswed etc.

45 min. snehan & swedan 2-3 times a day. Criteria & parameters for assessment. Respiration rate, pulse rate, Duration of bahi kumbhak, purak, rechak, expiration, were noted.

Peak flow meter reading, sphygmomano meter reading. 40 mm endurance list chest expansion capacity of speech, tendency of perspiration, cough, black onts, nansia were assessed.

Conclusion : Where snehan swedan was administered in acute condition, symptoms were relieved in some patients while in some patients there was relief in acute condition followed by increase in cough neusea.

Patients there was relief in acute condition followed by increase in cough & nausea.

Better results were achieved in the acute conditions with the help of internal medication and internal snehan.

This treatment is more effective when the patient is not in the acute condition and after vaman chikitsa to avoid recurrence of the disease.

Snehan swedan are effective treatments in alleriation of both vata & kapha who have naturally contradictory properties.

The role of virechana chikitsa in udar vyadhi (Ascitis)

The main aim is to study udar vyadhi in detail especially with reference to virechan chikitsa & to co-relate dosha - sanchaya to virechan chikitsa which is the most important part of udar chikitsa.

Patients having accumulation of fluid/doshas in the peritoneal cavity were undertaken.

60% patients responded fevorably But there were limitation as-

Age (above 60 years), liver cirrthosis, advanced jatodakavastha (accumulation of fluid)

To study the efficacy of anuvasan Basti & Pichu during the ninth month of pregnancy according to Garbhini Paricharya (Ante natural care) explained by charaka.

According to Garbhini paricharya medicated oil should be used for the purpose of Anuvasan basti & pichu. This oleation helps in alleviating vata, building up strength, gives proper direction to apan vayu (type of vata). It also helps in stimulating proper contraction.

Bala tail was used for anuvasan basti & was administered twice in a week from the beginning & ninth month upto the stage & labour.

Bala Tail was used for pichu due to this treatment the total duration of labour period was reduçed & in some cases it helped to avoid epiziotomy.

Great relief was observed in symptoms like lumbar pain, frequent micturation & weakness.

To study the efficacy of tinospora (cordifolia) Guduchi - Ashwagandha (withenia somnifera) siddhia kshir basti in asthimajajagata - vata with special reference to prushtnavansha sandhi.

Symptoms like joint - pain, weakness, insomnia, muscular weakness, pain at lumbar region, porosity of bones etc. are absorved in asthimajjagata vata.

Guduch - Ashwagandha siddha kshir basti was administered daily for fifteen days.

Group I - 20 patients - Basti only.

Group II - 10 patients - Mahayogaraj guggul tabs only.

Group III -10 patients - Basti + Mahayograj guggul tabs.

Maximum results were obtained in Group 3 due to adiministration of basti along with oral treatment.

Role of Shirodhara in Nidranash

In last few decades, human psyche has failed to come up with rapid change of life style and very fast progress of technology. Hence nidranaṣh (insomnia) is the most observed mental health problem.

Aim of this project was to study the role of shirodhara in management of nidranash.

Criteria for selection :

Patients with history of nidranash, at least for a month and also having associated symptoms like body - ache, dizziness, indigestion, dryness, weight loss etc. were included in the study.

Total number of patients :

Forty (IPD + OPD) divided in

Group (I) Shirodhara - 30 patients

Group (II) With placebo - 10 patients (wheat flour 2 tabs at bed time)

Oil used for shirodhara - sesame oil.

Follow up : Daily for 7 days.

Criteria for Diagnosis :

Following investigations were undertaken to exclude other pathology -

HB % total WBC count, differential WBC Count, ESR, PVC, urine routine and microscopic, BSL.

Total effect of Therapy :

a. Complete Remission : 75% to 100% relief in chief complaints and improvement in sleeping upto 6 hours at night.

b. Markedly improved : 50% to 75% relief in chief complaints and improvement in sleeping upto 4 to 6 hours.

c. Improved : Upto 50% relief in chief complaints and improvement in sleeping hours.

d. Unchanged : No improvement in complaints and sleeping hours.

Conclusion :

Shirodhara with sesame oil effective in nidranash showing improvement in total sleep period and also the pattern of sleep.

Efficacy of Uttarbasti in infertility

This project was undertaken to study the efficacy of uttarbasti along with internal medication in infertility.

Materials and Method :

Case history was taken and examinations were done as follows:

1. Mensrual history.
2. Marital status
3. Use of contraceptives
4. H.S.G. in females
5. Semen examination in males

Swatashekhar 250 mg. once a day with milk was used for internal medication. 500 gm. sesame oil was processed with 100 gm. Daruharidra, Haridra (Curcuma longa) and Devdar. This processed sesame oil was used for the purpose of uttar basti.

Total number of patients : 35

Observation : 17, out of 35 patients got conceived (48.50%)

Conclusion : Good results were observed in infertility due to conditions such as :

1. Small size of uterus.
2. Small size of os.
3. Unovalatory cycle etc.

Efficacy of snehan on the wound of Episiotomy :

This project was undertaken to study the efficacy of external snehan in wound healing of episiotomy.

Materials and Methods : Wound was examined from the second day of labour. Autoclaved warm sesame oil was used for parishek snehan (10-12 cc at a time) The wound was cleaned and dressed with a gauze piece soaked in sesame oil twice a day. The above procedure was repeated daily for seven days in this group (group I) The second group (group II) in which snehan therapy was not applied was also kept under observation for seven days.

Conclusion :

Inflammation was reduced on 3rd day in Group I and on 5th day of Group II. Alleviation of pain was observed earlier in Group I.

Role of Upanah Swed in sandhigata vata (Osteoarthritis)

Upanah swed plays an important role in treatment of sandhigatavata as it is one of the types of vatavyadhi.

Selection of patients :

Patients suffering from sandhigata vata with symptoms such as oedema, pain, restricted & painful movements at joint regions were selected.

Number of patients : 50

Total duration of the treatment : 7-31 days.

Types of Swedan :

Upanah swed was selected on criterion of various symptoms. Yogaraj Guggul was advised in the dose of 125 mg. 3 times a day with warm water to patients in whom internal medication was necessary.

Conclusion :

Prevalance of this disease is more in age group between 50-70 years.

Most affected joints are knee joint (66%) and ankle joint (28%)

Better results are observed when swedan chikitsa is supplemented with internal medication.

18.
GLOSSARY

18. Glossary

Avagaha sweda

Charaka has described thirteen types of sweda (fomentation). Avagaha sweda is one of the types of sweda. In this type of sweda patient is made to lie down in a tub full of vata alleviating decoction. It may be local (sit'z bath)/complete. According to 'Bhavprakash' - patient is made to lie down in such a way that only area of 6 fingers above umbilicus remains below the decoction. At the same time a drip of decoction is held over the patients shoulders. This sweda is useful mainly for renal colic, low backache. The duration should be of half an hour.

Ayoga :

Various criteria's for proper/improper therapies in panchakarma have been described in the texts. The criteria of improper completion of therapies can further be classified as ayoga and atiyoga. When the dose of the medicine administered is less or it is not administered in the proper way, proper results are not obtained and it leads to various complications according to the various therapies.

Atiyoga :

The criteria of improper completion of therapies can further be classified as ayoga and atiyoga. Administration of medicine in improper manner causes excessive bouts i.e. excessive emaciation and leads to various complications. This condition is termed as Atiyoga.

Upanaha sweda (poltis) :

This is a type of sweda. A paste of vata alleviating medicines is made in 'kanji'. Rock salt is added to it. This is tied on the particular affected part. This helps reducing pain and contracture in the particular region.

Manda :

Yavagu is one of the preparations used in sansarjan krama. Manda, Peya and vilepi together constitute the yavagu. The proportion is uncooked rice is same in all the three preparations i.e. it should be 1/4th of the rice needed in the normal diet of a person. While preparing manda, the proportion of medicated water should be fourteen times that of the rice. When the rice is cooked only the liquid portion is used for the diet and is termed as 'Manda'.

Peya :

The proportion of medicated water is six times that of the rice in case of peya. After the rice is cooked the portion of liquid should be more and along with it little portion of cooked rice is also taken. This is termed as peya.

Vilepi :

The proportion of medicated water is four times that of the rice. After the rice is completely cooked, the portion of cooked rice should be more and the portion of liquid should be comparatively less. This preparation is termed as vilepi. As the proportion of medicated water is consecutively less in manda, peya and vilepi they are more heavy to digest respectively. Hence in sanjarjan kram, the sequence of diet is manda-peya and later on vilepi, instead of rice. Various other cerals like wheat etc. can also be used for preparing yavagu.

❖❖❖

GLOSSARY

Introduction :

Terms used	Meaning
Kayachikitsa	Medicine
Kaumarbhritya tantra	Paediatrics
Grihachikitsa	Treatment based on planets.
Shalakya tantra	Otolaryngology & Ophthalmology
Shalya tantra	Surgery
Visha tantra	Toxicology
Rasayan	The treatment which increases the immunity & longevity
Vajikaran	Treatment dealing with sexual sphere & organs
Styaan	Sticky
Pichchil	Smooth & Slippery
Koshtha	Superficial level (in relation to the site for elimination of doshas)
Shakha	Deeper level (in relation to the site for elimination of doshas)
Rasa	First dhatu formed after digestion of food
Rakta	Second dhatu- blood

Mansa	Third dhatu - Muscle tissue
Meda	Fourth dhatu - Adipose tissue
Asthi	Fifth dhatu - Bone tissue
Majja	Sixth dhatu - Bone marrow
Shukra	Seventh dhatu
Doshas	Basic biological humors conducting the bodily functions
Dhatus	Substances which hold the body & perform basic functions
Aam	Undigested substances causing vitiation of other body constituents
Koshtha	Superficial level (in relation to the site for elimination of doshas)

Panchakarma & You :

Term used	Meaning
Karmas	Procedures
Padabhyang	Feet massage
Pratimarsha nasya	Type of nasya having dose of 2 drops in each nostril
Matra-basti	Type of Sneha basti (enema) having dose of 60 gm.

Constitution :

Terms used	Meaning
Prakruti	Individual constitution
Doshas	Basic biological humors conducting bodily functions
Gunas	Characteristics

Panchakarma :

Terms used	Meaning
Dhoomapan	Inhalation of medicinal fumes
Sansarjan krama	Dietetic regimen to be followed after some procedures
Santarpan	Dietetic regimen which provides nourishment
Gunas	Characteristics
Yavakshar	A kind of kshar
Yusha	Soup of various pulses
Yavagu	Soup of various cereals
Kshar	Corrosive alkaline material
Pichchil	Smooth & slippery
Vataj shirorog	Head-ache due to dominance of vitiated vata
Dhoomayantra	Special apparatus used for inhalation of medicinal fumes

Jalauka shodhana	Purification of jalaukas (leeches)
Shatadhaut ghrita	Ghee which has been purified hundred times
Aasthapana basti	Decoctional enema
Abhyang	Oleation
Rakta	Blood
Rookshana	Therapy which alleviates unctuousness
Anjan	Application of medicines in the eye
Raktatisaar	Presence of blood in stools during diarrhoea
Deepan	Increase in digestive power
Stambhana	Substances causing alleviation of any discharge or flow from the body.
Shukra	Seventh Dhatu
Bahupittakamala	Jaundice due to increase of pitta
Shakhashrita kamala	Jaundice due to obstruction of pitta
Strotasas	Systems
Pakvashaya	Large intestine
Kleda	Improperly digested sticky substances
Pratishyaya	Rhinitis
Abhishyandi	Substances causing indigestion & generation of kleda

Vatavyadhi	Various vata predominant diseases
Pranavayu	Type of vata
Upanah swed	Type of swedan where paste of swedan substances is tied
Pradhaman nasya	Type of nasya using powdered medicines having strong potency
Allied Karma :	
Terms used	**Meaning**
Sneha	Unctuous substances
Samhitas	Texts
Dhara	Flow of a liquid in a drip
Kshara Karma	Use of alkaline material as a treatment
Sukumar	Delicate
Disease & Panchakarama :	
Terms used	**Meaning**
Vidahi	Property which causes indigestion & burning sensation
Asbhishyandi	substance causing indigestion & generation of kleda.
Dhoomapan	Inhalation of medicinal fumes
Mansa dhatu	Muscle tissue
Anuvasan basti	Enema of unctuous material

Nirooha basti	Decoctional enema
Virechan	Purgation
Pichcha basti	Enema of substances having smooth & slimy characteristics
Vaman	Emesis
Langhan	Fasting / intake of light diet
Pachan	Digestion
Aam	Undigested material causing vitiation of body constituents
Nasya	Errhine therapy
Raktamokshan	Blood letting
Snehan	Oleation
Swedan	Fomentation
Dhoom nasya	Nasya using medicinal fumes
Saamavastha	Presence of aam in body constituents.
Niramavastha	Absence of aam in body constituents.